SERVING CHRIST

A FAMILY AFFAIR

SERVING CHRIST

A FAMILY AFFAIR

Terry L. & Beverly Miethe

COLLEGE PRESS
PUBLISHING COMPANY
Joplin, Missouri

Copyright © 1995
College Press Publishing Company

Printed and Bound in the
United States of America
All Rights Reserved

Scripture quotations are from the *New American Standard Bible*, © 1960, 1962, 1963, 1968, 1971, 1972, 1973, 1975, and 1977 by The Lockman Foundation. Used by permission.

Library of Congress Cataloging-in-Publication Data

Miethe, Terry L., 1948–
    Serving Christ: a family affair / Terry L. & Beverly Miethe.
      p. cm.
    Includes bibliographical references (p. 215).
    ISBN 0-89900-730-9 (pbk.)
      1. Family—Religious life.   2. Christian education—Home training.   3. Witness bearing (Christianity)
I. Miethe, Beverly, 1948–   . II. Title.
BV4526.2.M45 1995
248.4—dc20   95-140
                                                                           CIP

Dedicated to:

𝔅ritain 𝔄very 𝔐iethe,

with the prayer, and in the hope,
that you will carry on the tradition of
Christian ministry in our family!

We believe God has a purpose for your life . . .
discover it . . . fulfill it . . .
and you will be the richest of men!

Other Works by Terry L. Miethe

Living Your Faith: Closing the Gap Between Mind and Heart, 1993.

Why Believe? God Exists! Rethinking the Case for God and Christianity, with Gary R. Habermas, 1993.

Does God Exist? A Believer and an Atheist Debate, with Antony G.N. Flew, 1991.

"The Universal Power of the Atonement," chapter four in *The Grace of God, The Will of Man*, 1989.

The Compact Dictionary of Doctrinal Words, 1988.

A Christian's Guide to Faith & Reason, 1987.

Did Jesus Rise from the Dead? The Resurrection Debate, with Gary R. Habermas and Antony G. N. Flew, 1987; paperback edition 1989.

The Philosophy and Ethics of Alexander Campbell: From the Context of American Religious Thought, 1800 to 1866, 1984.

The New Christian's Guide to Following Jesus, 1984.

Augustinian Bibliography, 1970-1980: With Essays on the Fundamentals of Augustinian Scholarship, 1982.

"Atheism: Nietzsche," chapter six in *Biblical Errancy: An Analysis of its Philosophical Roots*, 1981.

Thomistic Bibliography, 1940-1978, with Vernon J. Bourke, 1980.

Reflections, Vol. I, 1980; Vol. II, 1983; Vol. III, 1988; Vol. IV, 1988.

The Metaphysics of Leonard James Eslick: His Philosophy of God, 1976.

Friedrich Nietzsche & the Death of God: The Rejection of Absolutes, 1973.

Table of Contents

Preface 9

Introduction 15

  1. A Positive Idea of God 19

  2. The Family in the Bible 37

  3. What Makes a Home Christian? 51

  4. The Family First in the Church 65

  5. The Family and Worship 85

  6. Church Leaders and Their Families 101

  7. Parenting: Some Practical Suggestions 111

  8. Nurturing Children in the Lord 127

  9. The Family that Prays *and* Plays Together 145

10. The Family Today 163

11. The Family and Ministry 183

12. The Family, Christian Education, & the World . . . 195

Epilogue: The Family, Ministry, & the Future 207

Select Bibliography 215

About the Authors 219

Preface[1]

Serving Christ: A Family Affair is a celebration of the family, especially the Christian family. There are so many pressures and negative forces working on the family these days. We know this. But it is time for a loud and clear affirmation to ring out over the land: in spite of more than two decades of pronouncements of doom, THE FAMILY IS STILL ALIVE AND WELL! In 20 years no one has come up with an alternative foundation for society — and no one will. Yes, the family as an institution could be stronger and healthier — and needs to be. Yet there are tens of thousands of strong families across America.

We are told that there are over six million children in America living in homes that have suffered divorce.[2] There are also millions of children living in relatively stable homes as well. But we must not, dare not, ignore these divided families and the families in crisis. We must do all that we can to help these unsuccessful individuals to be able to form, or reform strong family units. We cannot go back to the 1950s or 60s, but we don't think that is the answer anyway. There were large numbers of

---

[1]NOTE: Throughout, we quote or make reference to various sources that relate to a point being made in this book. However, the fact that these sources are used to illustrate a particular point in this book should not be taken in any way as a "blanket" endorsement of the source; or, in other words, it should not be assumed that we accept or agree with every point or position taken in the source sighted. For example, even among Christians there exists a wide range of views about role relationships in marriage.

[2]CBS Evening News, 5 March 1995.

families in trouble then, too. All of us who were alive in the 50s and 60s know this. A "glorified" view of the past will never be the answer for the future. We can, and must, move ahead. How? By strengthening the institution of the family! Our solution is not simple nor is it naive.

We must pay the price, whatever it may be,[3] to reclaim as many of these individuals from divided families as we possibly can. Though not often practiced, it has been clear from the beginning of America, that it is much wiser to use our resources of democracy on the "front end"; i.e., the integrity of the family, education, moral training, etc.; rather than on paying for the crime, prisons, etc., that result from the disintegration of family and society. In other words, it is far less expensive to "pay" to give society a sound foundation, than to try to repair it after it is broken! In fact, if there is an "underlying" purpose for this book, that is it.

But the "blind can never lead the blind."[4] *We believe that Christian families are the answer! If* Christian families

---

[3]Alexander Campbell (1788-1866) realized that to accomplish his religious revolution one had to engage in a reformation of education. He said, "Of all earthly objects [education] is the chief concern." And, "next to the gospel, this is the most important of human concerns and interests." *The Millennial Harbinger* [*MH*] (1838), pp. 92, 204. He wrote, "If it should yet require the appropriation of a hundred millions [sic] of dollars to bring a good education to the door of every American citizen, to compel the education of all, when it cannot otherwise be accomplished, we would be wanting in the grand elements of a Christian community, nay, of a wise and prudent and moral people, if we should not, situated as we are, make vigorous efforts to raise that sum, and devote it to that use. I know no value in money beyond food and raiment, except so far as it puts within our grasp the means of instruction." *MH* (1837), p. 64. See also, "Value of Education and "Education" in *MH* (1848), pp. 538-539. Alexander Campbell, *The Millennial Harbinger,* Reprinted and distributed by College Press Publishing Co., Joplin, MO, 1987.

[4]See Terry L. Miethe, "Beware of 'One-eyed' Kings," Chapter 11 in *Living Your Faith: Closing the Gap Between Mind and Heart* (Joplin, MO: College Press Publishing Co., 1993), pp. 109-118.

Preface

understood how to martial their families as a ministering force to impact other families, we could begin to reclaim the institution of the family — and even society itself. We could and we must. That is what this book is all about — the great privilege and serious responsibility of the Christian family to worship the Lord and to model what it is to be a "family" to the world around them.

We have wanted to write this book for a long time. Frankly, one of the reasons we waited was that we wanted to make sure we had the "right" to write. More than "academic credentials" or "ministerial experience" is important to a book like this. We did not want to write on something we really didn't know all that much about — as so many do. In other words, we wanted to live enough of the "story" of our family to see how it was going to turn out. Through God's grace, we have the great blessing of a Christian family. We rejoice in this blessing and the privilege of sharing it!

Now, the time has come. In 1994, we celebrated the twenty-fifth anniversary of our marriage. Though we cannot think of any particular individual, there were probably some who said it wouldn't last. Well, it has lasted and *will continue to last!* We *are* in love, more in love today than when we were married. Marriage is the most sacred bond and wonderful relationship two persons can share. Through it, they become one in the eyes of God! Early in our marriage, we had the privilege of actually sitting around the very table at which Martin Luther sat when he said of marriage, "There is no more lovely, friendly and charming relationship, communion or company than a good marriage."[5] We could not agree more!

This 25th anniversary year has been a really wonderful year: We saw the marriage of our only son, John Hayden,

---

[5]Martin Luther, *Table Talk* (1509), p. 292.

Serving Christ: A Family Affair

to a beautiful Christian young lady named Lisa Nicole;[6] the birth of our first grandson, Britain Avery Miethe; and the rededicating of our love and life to each other and to Christ! Sitting in our living room, John Hayden and Nicole told us they wanted to marry. Nicole looked at us, and with tears in her eyes, said, "I love him with all my heart." Instantly, we both had tears as well! We love and respect our son. We know him well enough to know that for him to choose Nicole, she must be a special person indeed! Terry asked them only one question, "Can you grow old together?"

John and Nicole have grown up in a "throw-away" generation. The deeply ingrained attitude seems to be, "If it's broken, just throw it away. Why bother trying to fix it?" All around them is a generation that uses up mates as often, sometimes more often, than it does cars! This must stop. But it will only stop if the Christian church helps the generations coming up to understand that love and lust are not the same, to value themselves and others as being created in God's image, to "revere" promise keeping and to understand commitment! But before the church can have such an impact on society it must teach its own that serving Christ is a family affair.

You want to know the key to a marriage that will last and fulfill? Tender compassionate *love* and *communication* in words and with deeds! Communication is necessary to convey the love, to explain it, and to reinforce it. You cannot, must not, expect a mate to read your mind and just "know" you love him or her. We all need verbal reassurance *often*! There is no substitute for communication of love in a marriage that is to be a union of two souls.

---

[6]Throughout this book, Nicole, although actually our daughter-in-law, is simply referred to as our daughter — she is so very much a part of our family.

Indeed, to the extent that you communicate your love you will grow closer together.

The longer the period you do not communicate the farther apart you will become. It should be no surprise that there is such a high rate of divorce after children leave the nest. When spouses spend literally years communicating almost exclusively through, or for, their offspring and all of a sudden the children are gone, the stark reality that they have nothing in common — and haven't had for years — hits them like the proverbial "ton of bricks." For heaven's sake, talk to each other openly and honestly often![7]

Our first twenty-five years have been far from "perfect." In writing this book, we are not claiming to have "arrived." But we are definitely "on the road" and making progress. We are reminded of John Locke's insightful words, "All men are liable to error; and most men are, in many points, by passion or interest, under temptation to it."[8] We agree and are certainly not exceptions. But we hope as we have "matured," that our "passions" are more directed toward Christ and our "temptations" are more controlled by knowledge of and commitment to Him.

---

[7] See H. Norman Wright, *Communication-Key to Your Marriage* (Glendale, CA: Regal Books, 1974). Book contains a teacher-leader's guide and a class text. John Powell, *The Secret of Staying in Love* (Niles, IL: Argus Communications, 1974). The book says, "The secret of staying in love is communication. Indeed, our greatest gift to each other is a gift of self through the honest sharing of feelings and emotions." Paul A. Cedar, *Seven Keys to Maximum Communication* (Wheaton, IL: Tyndale House Publishers, 1980).

[8] John Locke (1632-1704), *Essay Concerning Human Understanding*, (1690), Book IV, Ch. 20, Sec. 17. Locke worked on this important "essay" for almost 20 years before he published it. The critical edition is: *Essay Concerning Human Understanding* in The Clarendon Edition of the Works of John Locke, Edited with an Introduction, Critical Apparatus and Glossary by Peter H. Nidditch (Oxford: At the Clarendon Press, 1975).

Serving Christ: A Family Affair

Along the way in our marriage, we have learned some important and powerful lessons. We know we will continue to learn. Some of the lessons are: (1) If forgiveness is a central theme of the Gospel and essential to understanding and living the Christian life, the ability to forgive is "even more" essential in a marriage that will last. (2) We have learned time and again that: Love comes out of commitment . . . not commitment out of love." (3) "Being supportive in any relationship essentially means to actively encourage the fulfillment of the other." And, (4) "The richest of marriages is the one that shares a dream."[9] We thank God everyday for giving us each other, and we thank Him for each day together. We wish you the fullness that can only come from loving each other and serving each other as you love and serve Him! For serving Christ is truly a family affair!

—Terry L. & Beverly Miethe
16 April 1995
The Festival of the Resurrection of Jesus

---

[9]Terry L. Miethe, *Reflections*, Volume One, 1980.

Introduction

From Eden to eternity, from the creation of the first Adam to the reign of the last Adam; from Deuteronomy 6 to Ephesians 6; God makes it clear that serving Him is a family affair. Since our early days in graduate school, we have been interested in the family as a force for real ministry. We remember fondly when a pilot for a major airlines, a member of our church and a close friend, took us to a large hole in the ground in a posh suburb on the northern edge of the Chicago area. There he showed us the foundation of a house his family was building, a very expensive home in those days and even more so today.

Our pilot friend surprised us by asking point-blank, "Should we as a Christian family own such an expensive home?" Our answer was a rather immediate "Yes." The answer came so quickly because we knew this family was truly a family of God. We knew that every aspect of their lives, of their family (including their possessions), were used in ministry for the Lord. Though they were not formally educated in theology, we never left their home but that we knew more about ministry, understood more clearly the wonderful privilege the Christian family has to minister to others and by so doing to build the kingdom of God! This family modeled Christianity to everyone with whom they came into contact.

Recently, *Parenting* magazine reported a survey. One of the questions asked which television show most accurately reflects your family. Forty percent said *Roseanne!*[1] Growing up in the midwest, we knew a family (or two) like the family of "Dan and Roseanne Conner," but they would hardly have been considered models. Just the opposite! Surely the people responding to this survey were not saying the "Conner" family was a "role model" for their families, just that this TV family was the most accurate *representation* of how their family actually functioned. But which is worse? How sad, tragic really! If this is the case, it doesn't take a genius to see why our families and our society are in such trouble.

Oprah Winfrey dedicated an entire hour show to the cast of *Roseanne*. She referred to the "Conners" as "America's most dysfunctional family." Now, this has the ring of truth. Yet watching TV, it would be really hard to figure out which show actually contributed most to the decline of the family. There are *so many* prime candidates! Viewing those growing legions of talk and cop shows, one has to wonder if there is a "functional" family in the land. We wonder which is worse: (1) that so many families are willing to go on TV and expose themselves, (2) that they don't seem to realize what they are saying about themselves, (3) that the "guardians" of our airwaves allow such garbage on TV; or (4) that evidently there are enough people watching that these shows keep growing like so many deadly bacteria.

We used to think soap operas were high on the list of the most immoral shows on TV. Now, we are beginning to think a strong case can be made that the soaps led the decline, and the talk shows may be the final cause of the fall of the American family. One thing is certain. Perhaps, we should get this out of the way at the very beginning: *Christian parents must not ignore their responsibility to*

---

[1]Reported on National Public Radio on 28 September 1994. To this question 27% answered *Leave it to Beaver*, and 7% said *The Simpsons*.

Introduction

control, censor, and guide the children in choosing TV programs. Not even all so-called "children's programs" are acceptable to Christian parents. The most dangerous thing about TV is very subtle — that we will allow it to monopolize our time and crowd out other real adventures we could be having with our children. One of the most important actions we could take to strengthen our families is to greatly limit TV watching by all members.

There is a disease consuming our world today: A disease more insidious than materialism, more ravishing than cancer, more dangerous than bigotry, more infectious than racism. That disease is MEDIOCRITY. There is a real danger it will destroy our nation, emasculate the church, and become a way of life for individual Christians. It is dissolving our families. But it will never conquer the gospel of Christ!

But the purpose of this book is not to argue that the family is disintegrating, or to chart this disintegration in our society, or even to try to suggest some "quick fixes" to the problem. Rather, it is about the fact that *the family is a divine institution* and therefore a wonderful gift from God. It is about *the challenge to reclaim our families as God's instrument to be salt, light, and leaven in our society.* In short, it is *about empowering the Christian family to be God's agent in our world as He intended.*

It is also, at least indirectly, about the fact that when the Christian family assumes its proper place in our churches and society, it can and will be *the* instrument to rejuvenate both. When serving Christ truly becomes a family affair our churches and our society will improve! *Without question, the largest "untapped" resource, the greatest unused power for ministry is the Christian family!*

CHAPTER ONE
A Positive Idea of God

The place to begin a book about the family and ministry is with God, the Father. This is really an essential starting point. All things begin and end with God! We are reminded of Wordsworth's lines, ". . . But when the great and good depart, What is it more than this — That Man who is from God sent forth, Doth yet again to God return? . . ."[1] Different people have different views as to the "heart" or essence of Christianity. Some say it's all about evangelism, or the Bible, or doing good things. But GOD IS — and this is the most incredible, overwhelming realization a person can have.

Life is a *quest* — what a beautiful word — to find meaning and purpose. Real meaning and true purpose come only from God. Having found Him, Christianity unfolds as a lifetime of trying to know Him better and of trying to grow closer and closer to Him. So many have, not necessarily a wrong view of Christianity, but a woefully inadequate and shallow view. They think the essence of faith is in *not* doing certain things. Often without knowing it, they view the faith and ethics almost always in the negative. But as Christians, we are ethical by what we *do*, not by what we don't do. As Christians,

---

[1] "A power is passing from the earth / To breathless Nature's dark abyss; / But when the great and good depart, / What is it more than this — / / That Man who is from God sent forth, / Doth yet again to God return? — / Such ebb and flow must ever be, / Then wherefore should we mourn?" *Lines on the Expected Dissolution of Mr. Fox* by William Wordsworth (1770-1850).

Serving Christ: A Family Affair

we have the glorious privilege of striving to live out the very character of God one with another! What a magnificent thought.

The Bible teaches that God is intimately related to us — or wants to be — and that we are intimately related to Him — or should be! It presents God as a living, personal, loving, Supreme Being who is our Heavenly Father, and was vitally interested enough in our daily lives to send His Son to come and live with us.

> Contemporary Christianity needs more theology! Not just the theology of the study and the library, but that truly biblical theology which makes God real, in experience as well as in theory. This was the theology of Moses and Isaiah, of Paul and John. Can anything less claim the title of "biblical theology"?

So writes R. T. France in his book, *The Living God*.[2] Before we can really understand the nature or importance of the family, or how God intended the family to serve Him and minister to others, God must be real to us, real in *our* experience, not just in theory or in our "belief system." France reminds us quite correctly that Moses, Isaiah, Paul and John could tell us about God in the Scriptures (the basis for all Christian theology) because He was intimately real to them.

France goes on to say that even though "a recent survey found that 97% believe in God. . . . Yet . . . in America, God is dead." France is asserting that this is true, "As far as the ordinary man in the pew is concerned, . . . They have no place for God; not practically at any rate."[3]

---

[2] R.T. France, *The Living God: A Personal Look at What the Bible Says About God* (Inter-Varsity Press, London, 1970), p. 8. This is one of the best little "introductions" to theology we have ever seen.

[3] France, *Ibid.*, pp. 9, 10. France's book was published in October 1970, but if anything this claim is more true today. Many more surveys have been done; e.g., a very famous philosopher/theologian

A Positive Idea of God

In other words, how are our ordinary "daily lives" affected by our belief? We contend that this fact — that God no longer really impacts many lives on a daily basis; and, therefore, that God does not seem real[4] — is one very major factor in the decline of the American family!

D. Martyn Lloyd-Jones, in his exceptional *Studies in the Sermon on the Mount*, points out the importance of realizing the power of the personal presence of God in our daily lives, and in prayer. In Matthew chapter 6 we have ". . . what we may well call a picture of the Christian living his life in this world in the presence of God, in active submission — a difficult term for us, even with respect to Him — to God, and in entire dependence upon Him." Here Jesus tells us that "the ultimate choice is always the choice between pleasing self and pleasing God."

> *The supreme matter in this life and world for all of us is to realize our relationship to God.* One almost apologizes for making such a statement, and yet I suggest that the greatest cause of all our failures is that we constantly forget our relationship to God. Our Lord puts it like this. We should realize that our supreme object in life should be to please God, to please Him only, and to please Him always and in everything. If that is our aim we cannot go wrong. Here, of course, we see the outstanding characteristic of the life of our Lord Jesus Christ. Is there anything that stands

---

named Gilson in an article "The Idea of God and the Difficulties of Atheism (1969) mentioned a poll in *Time* in 1965 where 97% of the U.S. population answered that they believed in God. Gilson wasn't impressed with this statistic when one examined the "quality" of that belief in God! See Miethe & Flew, *Does God Exist?: A Believer and an Atheist Debate*, San Francisco: Harper Collins, 1991, p. 277 (Chapter VIII, Note 4). Also referenced here is a 1992 *USA Today* newspaper poll which indicated that 95% of Americans believe in a Supreme Being. So What? See Miethe/Flew, p. 274 (Note 36).

[4]It is also interesting to note that when Hamilton, Van Buren, and others said this in the 1960's they were ridiculed and reviled.

out more clearly in His life? He lived entirely for God.[5]

There are two related truths for the Christian to remember which will help us live the Christian life: First, "We are always in the presence of God. We are always in His sight. He sees our every action, indeed our very thought." He knows your heart. You cannot deceive Him. If we realize that God is always with us, right beside us, closer than any friend, there will be things we simply would not want to do. It will not always be a matter of right and wrong, but of *appropriateness*.

Second, because God is constantly with us we can always talk to Him. We so take this for granted! We can talk to Him every minute of the day. We can ask Him for help with any problem. We can seek strength in any situation. In short, He is our constant companion. We must be open to that Presence. Here rests the true power of prayer![6] We will discuss the place of prayer more in chapter 8, "The Family that Prays and Plays Together." Why not take advantage of this help for you and for your family? These two "simple" realizations alone could revolutionize your family life!

There are many important aspects of the reality of God's presence in our lives. C.S. Lewis referred to God as "the Transcendental Interferer."[7] When was the last time *you*

---

[5]D. Martyn Lloyd-Jones, *Studies in the Sermon on the Mount*, Volume Two (Grand Rapids: Eerdmans, 1970), pp. 9,13, 14.

[6]Lloyd-Jones, *Ibid.*, p. 15. See also pages 21-32 on "How to Pray" and Miethe, *The New Christian's Guide to Following Jesus: A Manual for Spiritual Growth* (Minneapolis: Bethany House, 1984), "On Prayer," pp. 85-90.

[7]You should become acquainted with C.S. Lewis! You might want to start with *Mere Christianity* (1952), *Christian Reflections* (1967), *The Great Divorce* (1946) or *Till We Have Faces* (1956). All of Lewis' (1898-1963) books are helpful: his philosophical theology, e.g., *Allegory of Love* (1936), *The Problem of Pain* (1940), *A Preface to 'Paradise Lost'*

invited God to "interfere" in your life? "He is relentlessly, uncomfortably present in the sordid business of commerce and war, of loving, living, and dying"; of every aspect of our professional and personal lives.[8] He "interferes" because He loves us! If God is not "interfering" in your life and the life of your family — or you don't feel that He is — therein may be your greatest problem. Think about it.

God is Alive

God is a living, dynamic, loving Being. He is *Life*, the One who brought other living beings into existence and who keeps them in existence moment by moment.[9] He is actively present here and now. This is seen in the very name of God (Exod. 3:14, 15). The Hebrew word "to be" signifies a dynamic, active presence. God is actively related to us; and we, by being created in God's image, are actively related to God. Thus being created in God's image enables us to embrace *His* rationality and *His* freedom and *His* personality, and to have the capacity to love and for a spiritual relationship with God.[10] Christianity is

---

(1941), *The Abolition of Man* (1943), *Miracles* (1947), *Reflections on the Psalms* (1958), *Letters to Malcolm: Chiefly on Prayer* (1963); his children's stories, *The Chronicles of Narnia* are exceptional; his novels, *Out of the Silent Planet* (1938), *Perelandra* (1943), and *That Hideous Strength* (1945); his allegorical conversion journey in *The Pilgrim's Regress* (1933) or his autobiography *Surprised by Joy* (1955); or his personal struggle with grief and death in *A Grief Observed* (1960); etc.

[8] France, *Ibid.*, p. 11.

[9] Many Christians misunderstand the doctrine of creation. They seem to think God created the world and humankind and then "went off to play" as it were. This actually gives rise to a Deistic view of God. God did create the world in what we now view as some moment in the past; but He not only created it and us, He *sustains* it and us moment by moment in existence. We would not and could not now exist without His sustaining power. This is a very important, crucial insight. See Miethe & Habermas, *Why Believe? God Exists! Rethinking the Case for God and Christianity*, College Press, 1993.

[10] With regard to "God's Image Shines in Us," see Miethe, *Living Your Faith*, pp. 49-54.

not a way of life, *it is Life.* If you are not a Christian, you are not living, you are only existing.

An interesting thing happened to Paul and Barnabas in Lycaonia and Lystra. After healing a man "lame from his mother's womb, who had never walked" (Acts 14:8), the people said, "The gods have become like men and have come down to us" (vs. 11) and they began to call the two Zeus and Hermes. Even the priest of Zeus "wanted to offer sacrifice with the crowds" (vs. 13) to them. But when Paul and Barnabas heard of this "they tore their robes and begged the Lycaonians to "turn from these vain things to *a living God* WHO MADE THE HEAVEN AND THE EARTH AND THE SEA AND ALL THAT IS IN THEM" (Acts 14:15).

In Acts 17:22-31, Paul insists to the Athenians that God is not "unknown," but a living Creator, "Lord of heaven and earth" and "does not dwell in temples made with hands" (vs. 24). And, that this truth of the living God is sealed by and through the resurrection of Jesus from the dead:

> . . . God is now declaring to men that all everywhere should repent, because He has fixed a day in which he will judge the world in righteousness through a Man whom He has appointed, having furnished proof to all men by raising Him from the dead [emphasis added] (Acts 17:30-31).[11]

---

[11] See also I Corinthians 15:12-17 where Paul clearly makes the resurrection of Jesus the cornerstone of the faith and a matter of historical fact. It truly amazes us that scholars who call themselves "Christian" are still saying that the resurrection has no evidential value, that it is being misused when used to give support for the existence of God or the deity of Christ; e.g., Wayne W. Mahan, *Is It Possible to be Christian and Modern?*, in "IV The Vulgarization of the Resurrection of Jesus" (New York: University Press of America, 1993), pp. 27-28. Mahan says, "Just as the death of Jesus has been vulgarized so has the Resurrection of Jesus been vulgarized by being treated as a 'proof' for Christianity and immortality — as credulity desires" (p. 27). How ridiculous! The Apostle Paul thinks the resurrection constitutes proof (Acts 17:31). Mahan is a most unfortunate example of a person who thinks he

A Positive Idea of God

Read carefully through the book of Acts to see why and how the church grew and how strong was its prayer life![12] Also, the Thessalonians ". . . turned to God from idols to serve a *living and true God* (1 Thess. 1:9). The Bible clearly presents God as a living Being!

But perhaps the most important example is found in Hebrews (3:12; 9:14; 10:31) "which in particular makes use of the term 'the living God' to combat not idolatry *but a dead and formal religion, however pure and spiritual its belief in the one true God.*" [emphasis added] "To throw all that away, and return to a frustrating, ineffective rigmarole of 'dead works,' would be not only mad, but dangerous" writes R. T. France. He goes on to say something that should be preached long and loudly:

> A living relationship with a living God. That is Christianity; that is the heart of true religion. Christians are 'the temple of the living God' (2 Cor. 6:16), their very life derived through Christ from 'the living Father' (Jn. 6:57; cf. 5:26), and the undeniable reality of the change in their lives witnessing to the work of 'the Spirit of the living God' in them (2 Cor. 3:3); they press on undaunted by opposition and discouragement, because they have their 'hope set on the living God' (I Tim. 4:10), and because He is the living God their hope is not disappointed. These few

---

knows how to reason, but who — while well intentioned — confuses what he calls "circular reasoning" as well as "question-begging" in an inadequate analysis of the nature of "proof" and the use of reason which *can* support the claims of Scripture in the context of a worldview.

[12]You will want to examine the following texts: Acts 2:47; 5:14; 6:7; 9:31; 11:21-24; 12:2; 16:5; 19:20; 28:31 and of course their context, and the following prayers in Acts: 1:13-14, 15-26; 2:42-47; 3:1; 4:23-31; 6:4-7; 7:55-60; 8:9-25; 9:5, 6, 11, 36-43; 10:2-4, 9, 31; 12:5, 12-17; 13:2, 3, 43; 14:15, 23, 26; 16:13, 16, 25, 34; 20:36; 27:33, 35; 28:8, 15, 28. With regard to the Holy Spirit and the expansion of the church see Acts 1:2, 5, 8, 16; 2:4, 33, 38; 4:8; 5:3, 32; 6:5,10; 7:51, 55; 8:15, 17, 18, 19, 29; 9:17, 31; 10:19; 11:12, 28, 38, 44, 45, 47; 11:15, 16, 24; 12:2, 3; 13:9, 52; 15:8, 28; 16:6, 7; 19:2, 6, 21; 20: 23, 28; 21:4, 11; 28:25.

uses of the term 'the living God' . . . running richly through the whole of the New Testament [give] the conviction that God not only 'is', but 'lives', in dynamic and irresistible power, and in such a person-to-person relationship with His people that there is no room for idolatry or formal 'religion.' "[13]

Hebrews 11:10; 12:22; and 13:14 tell us that as Christians we have come to the city of the living God.[14]

Certainly, we could blame — and have — "old-fashioned liberal theology" and its modern counterpart for the powerlessness of so many churches. But no less blame *sticks* like ooze to those of us who have held to the form of biblical religion, with its doctrine of a personal and dynamic God, but by our lives have denied — or perhaps more accurately, never known — its power.[15] We firmly believe this "watering-down of God, and the consequent secularization of Christianity" is not only the reason so many churches are not growing, but is also at the heart of the problem with our Christian families today as well.[16]

---

[13]France, *Ibid.*, pp. 23,24.

[14]The basis for Augustine's (A.D. 354-430) famous book: *The City of God*. See Miethe, *Augustinian Bibliography, 1970-1980: With Essays on the Fundamentals of Augustinian Scholarship* (Westport, CT: Greenwood Press, 1982), 218 pages.

[15]We cry *often* over such a "dead and formal religion" which exists in large part in whole sections of the Restoration Movement even today! We have experienced it certainly on the "right" in churches of Christ, but in the "center" and on the "left" as well. Very recently (December 1994) we read an article which said that the Regional Minister, John Wolfersberger of the "Pacific Southwest Region" of the Christian Church (Disciples of Christ) stated that there were 131 churches in the region and that none had shown any growth since the previous Regional Assembly.

[16]When Joseph D. Stamey (Ph.D. Boston University), well-known United Methodist philosopher and theologian, and also an esteemed friend and colleague, read this paragraph he wrote, "Very much a Wesleyan theme that unfortunately many contemporary Methodists are unaware of."

A Positive Idea of God

God is a Person

It is most important for us to realize that God is a Personal Being. Much of the language the Bible uses personal categories when referring to God. What does it mean to be "personal"? Surely part of the story is:

> A person is a conscious being, one who thinks, feels, and purposes, and carries these purposes into action, one who has active relationships with others — you can talk to a person, and get a response; you can share feelings and ideas with him, argue with him, love him, hate him; you can know him, in a way which can only be described as "personal"![17]

It is so important for us to realize that God has all the attributes of "personhood." When this truth really soaks in we will realize that God can be our friend as any person can. The whole Bible tells us that God acts in relation to us His creation, that He is one with whom real relationships can be established. We have already hinted at the importance of this with regard to the potential power of His presence in our daily lives and in the power of prayer.

God is Love

He is a loving God, a God who pursues us, who shares our pain, who comforts us! The Prophet Hosea paints one of the most vivid pictures of God's love:

> ... for his prophetic calling involved him in nothing less than a broken marriage. Yet as he lavished his love on a worthless woman, and felt the bitterness of her desertion and adultery, and as his love still pursued her and took her back after it all, the whole episode was the most potent symbol of the love of

---

[17]France, *Ibid.*, pp. 19-20.

God, free and undeserved, yet spurned and suffering, and still pursuing His truant people with a faithfulness that knows no defeat, to restore them at last to the privileges of the covenant which they themselves have broken.[18]

This is true love! This is God's love! Hosea married a prostitute, Gomer. As Mark Berrier says in his helpful book, "The people of Israel were so sexually sinful that God did something very unusual to Hosea. He told Hosea to marry a prostitute and have children with her! . . . God loved Israel and Hosea loved Gomer, so God and Hosea felt the same kind of pain."[19] God wanted Hosea to *know* how He felt so that he could tell the people of Israel.

God chose Israel not because as a nation it was faithful, or morally attractive, or a great people; but because *He loved them* (Deut. 7:6-8; see also Ezekiel 16). God told Hosea to go get Gomer back as He planned to take Israel back from idols. It was totally undeserved, unconditional, free love; and, so it is with God and us! "Love" is the very nature or essence of God. God is love! Here is a great and glorious fact for if God did not love so, humankind would know nothing of His love!

God *chose* to love the Israelites. He *chose* to love us. We just respond, even if it is often late in the game. As Augustine said so beautifully:

> Late have I loved Thee, O Beauty so ancient and so new, late have I loved Thee! And behold, Thou wert within and I was without. I was looking for Thee out there, and I threw myself, deformed as I was, upon those well-formed things which Thou hast made. Thou wert with me, yet I was not with Thee. These

---

[18]*Ibid.*, pp. 85-86.

[19]Mark D. Berrier, Sr., *The Bible for Busy People. Book 1, The Old Testament* (Plano, TX: Seaside Press, Wordware Publishing, Inc., 1994), pp. 83-84.

things held me far from Thee, things which would not have existed had they not been in Thee. Thou didst call and cry out and burst in upon my deafness; Thou didst shine forth and glow and drive away my blindness; Thou didst send forth Thy fragrance, and I drew in my breath and now I pant for Thee; I have tasted, and now I hunger and thirst; Thou didst touch me, and I was inflamed with desire for Thy peace.[20]

How often do we, even as Christians, make the mistake of throwing ourselves on "those well-formed things," worshiping the creation, or created things — things made by Him — which, though beautiful actually take us further from Him, rather than bring us closer to Him?

To "love" and to "choose" go together. This is also true of human love, especially the love which culminates (to reach the highest point or degree; come to full effect) — yet, which really only begins — in marriage. Perhaps this is one of the reasons the Bible often relates God's love and marriage. Bear in mind, "Love comes out of commitment . . . not commitment out of love."[21] Also remember that it is this unconditional, steadfast, always faithful love of God in us that *should be required* to build a family and is certainly required to build a family that will minister as a family![22]

---

[20]Augustine (354-430), *Confessions*, X, 27.38; also in Vernon J. Bourke, *The Essential Augustine* (Indianapolis: Hackett Publishing Company, 1974), p. 148.

[21]So often, we are taught that "love" is a "romantic" or "physical attraction" thing, and we forget that it is really about *commitment*. This is why the "standard" marriage ceremony says "so long as ye both shall live" and "till death us do part." In reality, the relation between love and commitment is dialectical and complimentary. They come together and reinforce each other.

[22]None of us are perfect. This is why forgiveness, restoration, reconciliation are such important themes in the Bible!

Serving Christ: A Family Affair

God is Our Heavenly Father

The Bible portrays God as our Heavenly Father.[23] But herein lies the "rub" as it were.[24] Many of us have had such bad experiences with our earthly parents that we tend, at least psychologically, to see God in the same negative way we see a parent or parents. As J.B. Phillips reminded us, "Quite a lot of ordinary people, who would never dream of turning to psychiatry, nevertheless have an abnormal fear of authority, or of a dominating personality of either sex, which could without much difficulty be traced back to the tyranny of a parent." He goes on to say, "But what has this to do with an inadequate conception of God? This, that the early conception of God is almost invariably founded upon the child's idea of his father."[25] But the picture of God as Father — or Parent — as presented in the Bible is one of great love, giving, sacrifice, and compassion.

The character of God as Father is revealed exaltedly in the teaching of Jesus. Here we see for the first time God as Father of the individual believer and not simply of a nation. In Mark 14:36, Jesus first called God "Abba," the intimate Aramaic term for "Papa" — apparently the name a respectful son would have given his father in every stage of life, a term of affectionate respect — and gave the disciples authority to do so as well. The Lord's Prayer

---

[23]But not just in the sense of God as Creator. In other words, it is not just in the sense of God as being Creator or Father of us all that the term is used in the New Testament. Only believers can speak to God as "Abba" because we are sons, joint heirs with Jesus, and thus brothers in a relationship with Him and God as "Papa."

[24]We cannot spend time here discussing the "problem of religious language" and explaining analogy. Obviously, the term "father" is not used univocally when used of God and of man! See Norman L. Geisler, *Philosophy of Religion*, Part Three: God and Language (Grand Rapids: Zondervan, 1974), pp. 229-310.

[25]See J.B. Phillips, "Parental Hangover" in *Your God is Too Small* (New York: Macmillan Co., 1955), pp. 14-19.

A Positive Idea of God

(Matt. 6:9-13, Luke 11:2-4) in its Aramaic form probably began with "Abba." This breaks decisively with the remote and highly formal ways of addressing God used by the Jews of Jesus' day. The same term is used by believers of God in Romans 8:15 and Galatians 4:6. Paul sees in its use a symbol of the Christian's adoption as a son of God and his possession of the Spirit. It is because of our relationship to Jesus that we can use this intimate term, because we have been adopted as sons and daughters through Jesus we can use this personal term for God.

The clear implication of our being able to call God "Papa" is that God is concerned for the individual believer as an earthly father is, or should be, for his child. "If man leaves Eden under a curse, it is to a father's smile that the prodigal returns."[26] It is God's love that is supremely evident in His invitation to us to call Him "Our Father"! It is well also to bear in mind that the character of God as revealed in Scripture is not simply masculine. He is certainly not a chauvinistic deity. Bottom line: We must be to our children what God wants to be to us if we are going to be a "family of God"!

God Became Flesh

The Gospel of John declares, "And the Word became flesh and dwelt among us, and we beheld His glory, glory as of the only begotten from the Father, full of grace and truth" (1:14). And, "For God so loved the world, that He gave His only begotten Son, that whoever believes in Him should not perish, but have eternal life" (3:16). Colossians tells us, "For in Him all the fulness of Deity dwells in bodily form" (2:9).

Jesus is the actual physical embodiment of the very

---

[26]N.M. de S. Cameron, "The Fatherhood of God" in the *New Dictionary of Theology* edited by S.B. Ferguson, D.F. Wright, and J.I. Packer (Downers Grove, IL: InterVarsity Press, 1988), pp. 253-254.

Serving Christ: A Family Affair

nature of God. Most of what we can know about God positively comes from His revelation in the person and testimony of Jesus, His Son (John 1:18). This is the incredible fact of the New Testament which both awed and amazed its writers. We actually touched Him! (1 John 1:1,2). Jesus says, "He who has seen me has seen the Father" (John 14:9). The writer of Hebrews states that God used to speak to men by His word in the mouths of prophets but:

> . . . in these last days [He] has spoken to us in His Son, whom He appointed heir of all things, through whom also He made the world. And He is the radiance of His glory and *the exact representation of His nature*, and upholds all things by the word of His power. . . [emphasis added] (Heb. 1:2-3).

Amazing! Jesus is the image of the invisible God (Col. 1:15; 2 Cor. 4:4). What joy for humankind!

Our knowledge of God is inseparably related to our knowledge of Jesus! Eternal life is to know the only true God and Jesus Christ whom He sent to us (John 17:3).[27] He paid the price for our sins![28] He died on the cross to save us and rose to guarantee our new life! But if this great revelation is to be spread to all of humankind, we must be responsible for telling others the Good News.

Both of the divine institutions in the Bible (i.e., the church and the family) are responsible for spreading the word. This is why so much rests on us understanding the biblical function of the family as God's way to minister to others! Thus the word incarnate (Jesus) and the written

---

[27] Jesus also tells us in clear terms that, "no one comes to the Father, but through Me" (John 14:6).

[28] Again, as Joe Stamey so accurately commented in reading this, "I think it is a very large challenge to try to interpret this in our time which has almost lost any credible understanding of sin and — I'm afraid — even more of forgiveness."

A Positive Idea of God

word (the Bible) must be written on our hearts and minds and shared with others through the most natural vehicle available — the family! What could be more natural in God's economy than to see the Christian family as a ministering unit!

God as Spirit

But it is not enough to have an academic knowledge of the Bible. One of Terry's professors, a renowned evangelical scholar, used to say that you could know the Bible forwards and backwards, have it memorized word for word, and still go to Hell. We must have a personal knowledge of God through His Spirit. We must be born again (John 3:3-8, see also: 1 Peter 1:3; 1 John 4:7; Acts 2:38). Jesus promised that the Holy Spirit would come after He went to be with the Father (John 14:26; 15:26; 16:13, 14). First Corinthians 2:12 tells us that we have received "the Spirit who is from God, that we might know the things freely given to us by God."

We must claim all the gifts God has given us! We should search the Bible *diligently* (tirelessly) to find, and then claim, all the promises of God.[29] We must teach them *diligently* to our children (Deut. 6:4-9).[30] We must live according to the teachings of His Word, the Bible, and with the help of His Holy Spirit (John 14:16-17; 15:26; 16:7, 13-15). Of this we are sure, the Bible and the Holy Spirit will never conflict and we must judge the work of the Spirit by the revelation of God in the Bible.[31] But if we must judge what is claimed to be the work of

---

[29]See for example: W.T.H. Richards, *God's Great Promises: Fifty-two Bible Promises, one for each week of the year* (Nashville: Abingdon Press, 1973).

[30]See the section in chapter 2 on Deuteronomy 6:4-9.

[31]See Miethe, *Living Your Faith*, Chapter 8 "The Holy Spirit and Knowledge," pp. 85-91.

Serving Christ: A Family Affair

the Holy Spirit by what the Bible says, then it is also unquestionable that what is clearly, undeniably taught in Scriptures about the Holy Spirit must be true! So we must never be afraid to study the Scripture to discover the potential of the fullness of the Spirit in our lives! Thus to know God both the written word and the Spirit must play their part intimately in our lives and in our family life.

Earlier in this chapter, we said that Jesus tells us the ultimate choice is always between pleasing self and pleasing God. Very long ago St. Augustine, bishop of an obscure little town (Hippo) in North Africa, wrote a book entitled *The City of God*.[32] This was a defense of Christianity with hope for reconstructing the very fabric of the civilized world. This book, destined to become a literary classic of the western world, tells of two cities. The inhabitants of these two cities have two distinct views of morality. In the one, the very principle of morality, is the love of God. In the other, the very essence of evil, is selfishness (Phil. 3:17-20). Thus the human race can be divided into "two great camps," that of people who love the Lord and prefer God to self and that of people who prefer self to God.

Many of us were taught that the choice was between God and Satan. Not so! The choice is between God and Self.[33] The task of Satan is to influence us to choose Self. Augustine saw this clearly in his day. And we must see it clearly in our own! Yes, it is by the character of our wills, by the character of our dominate love, that WE are ultimately marked. How are YOU and your family marked?

---

[32] Written between A.D. 413-416. See Augustine, *Concerning The City of God Against the Pagans*, Edited by David Knowles (London: A Penguin Books Classic, 1972); or *The City of God*, an abridged version, edited, with an Introduction by Vernon J. Bourke (Garden City, NY: Image Books, 1958).

[33] Dr. Stamey's comment in reading this was, "Very important and profoundly true — as a close reading of Mark's Gospel establishes."

A Positive Idea of God

In which camp are you and your family to be found? Of course the question arises: Can we ever "reconstruct" the "very fabric of the civilized world" without reconstructing the family or having a strong family structure? We think not.

Chapter Two
The Family in the Bible

Some seem to wonder what the Bible says about a particular subject. "Does the Bible have any clear teaching on that subject?" In today's world many who ask the last question really want to rewrite the Bible in their own image! Often they are "uncomfortable" with what the Bible actually says — perhaps because it would mean a rather significant lifestyle change. We are reminded of the famous statement attributed to Mark Twain, "It ain't those parts of the Bible that I can't understand that bother me, it is the parts I do understand."[1] Make no mistake about it, the Bible is not silent about the family.[2] It tells us some very beautiful, important, and sometimes even "scary" things — scary because of the responsibility it puts on us as parents — about what God intended for the family. The family is one of the two divine institutions of God (the other being the church)!

Genesis 2:22-24

Man had been created in the midst of this wonderful and beautiful creation, but he was still not complete. God said it was not good for man to be alone, so he created a

---

[1] Alex Ayers, Editor, *The Wit and Wisdom of Mark Twain* (New York: Meridian Books, 1987), p. 24. Ayers comments in the context of this quote, "Mark Twain, the most irreverent of writers, was actually a very religious man, but he did not subscribe to any orthodox set of beliefs, and he did not believe that the Bible was literally the word of God."

[2] It is not our intent, nor is it possible in this short book, to look at every Scripture relating to the family or family relationships.

"helper *suitable for* [literally, "corresponding to"] him" (verse 18). Notice a "helper suitable for him," not a slave to him. Bone of his bone and flesh of his flesh. The King James has the unfortunate translation, "an *help meet* for him." Even the more modern "helpmate" does not really bear the meaning of what God was doing in the garden that day. The Living Bible says, "I will make a *companion* for him, a helper suited to his needs." Man was really incomplete. A part of him was missing! He needed a "completer." When that part came to him he would be made "whole." Pretty strong language, don't you think?

Then, the Scripture says, "For this cause a man shall leave his father and his mother, and shall cleave to his wife; and they shall *become one flesh*" (verse 24). Here we have perhaps the most succinct, but very telling definition of the family. Moses tells us both the beauty and the importance of marriage. Whether you are just contemplating marriage or whether you have been married for 25 years or more, you must understand the essential nature of the role of "companion" as the primary purpose of marriage. Not "companion" in the rather loose sense of a casual "traveling companion," but a companion who is part of the very being of the other!

"The woman was . . . formed for an inseparable unity and fellowship of life with man, and the mode of her creation was to lay the actual foundation of the moral ordinance of marriage."[3] God intended that marriage be the deepest corporeal (material, physical) and spiritual unity possible; "a vital communion of heart as well as of body."[4] It is striking how the words of Genesis 2:24 recur throughout the Bible. Jesus quotes this passage in Matthew 19:5 (and in Mark 10:7-8) and said, "Con-

---

[3]C.F. Keil and F. Delitzsch, *The Pentateuch* (Edinburgh: T. & T. Clark, 1866), p. 89.
[4]*Ibid.*, p. 90.

sequently they are no longer two, but one flesh. What therefore God has joined together, let no man separate" (Matt. 19:6, Mark 10:9). It is also quoted in Ephesians 5:31. Paul refers to Genesis 2:24 in 1 Corinthians 6:16.

Deuteronomy 6:4-9

Progress toward spiritual maturity depended, Moses obviously felt, upon the absorption and assimilation of certain truths by God's people, and he felt he must provide for their perpetuation. This he did by providing in this Scripture for the religious education of the family. "Hear, O Israel! The Lord is our God, the Lord is one! And you shall love the Lord your God with all your heart and with all your soul and with all your might" (Deut. 6:4-5). Moses' words here are known as the Hebrew *Shema*.[5] If we in the church today would follow the plan God revealed, we would have our answer regarding the "how" of spiritual maturity and the role of the family in it.

(1) Notice this Scripture starts by describing the attitude which the parents themselves must have toward God. Total commitment is required on the part of parents — to God first, to each other, and to the family. Love is the key to a vital relationship with God — and to each other. Love involves a commitment, a way of life that expresses wholehearted exclusive devotion! The expression of our love taps all the resources of heart, spirit, mind; all the inner strength that springs from our entire being as created in God's image. The realization that God

---

[5]The name of and the first Hebrew word of the classical Jewish declaration of faith found in Deut. 6:4. The last letters of the first and last words of this verse 4 are written in Hebrew Bibles in oversized script, thereby forming the Hebrew word "witness" to indicate that by this verse Jews testify to the oneness and uniqueness of God. By the second century A.D., the *Shema* prayer consisted of Deut. 6:4-9; 11:13-21; and Num. 15:37-41 together with special benedictions to be recited every morning and evening (based on Deut. 6:7).

Serving Christ: A Family Affair

loves us *must* permeate — "pervade, saturate, impregnate" — our entire pattern of living! This is the true basis of love and the foundation of "family" and home. Repeatedly we are to share with our children the fact that God has manifested His love in redeeming us through Jesus, just as He redeemed them from Egyptian bondage. By doing this we express our wholehearted devotion to God in daily life. This "manifestation" of the love of God for us, and ours for Him, *is* the foundation of the family and *will* transform it into a living witness!

This Scripture is quoted in Matthew 22:37; Mark 12:28-30 (where Jesus adds "with all your mind"[6]); and Luke 10:27. The husband and wife must first have dedicated to the Lord their total beings, every aspect of their personality. We really cannot accept Christ as *Savior* without accepting Him as *Lord* of our lives. It is very likely that if father and mother are not concerned about living for Christ minute by minute the rest of the family won't be either. This is the "great commandment." Jesus, in quoting this Old Testament passage, says this is the *first* responsibility of every Christian.

"And these words, which I am commanding you today, shall be on your heart" (Deut. 6:6). The word, "heart," is often used in the Bible as a metaphor for the mind, the reasoning ability of a person — that which makes a human, a human.[7] Thus, we have an injunction to keep this commandment of God for total commitment constantly in our minds. This presupposes a constant studying of God's Word by parents for their own growth and that of their children.

(2) Formal instruction of the children by the parents is

---

[6]For the implications of this addition see Miethe, "A Vision for the Church: Loving God With All Your Mind" in *One Body*, Vol. 11, No. 3 (Summer, 1994), pp. 11-13.

[7]With regard to what it means to be created in God's image, see Miethe's *Living Your Faith*, pp. 49-60.

The Family in the Bible

necessary. "And you shall teach them diligently to your sons . . ." (Deut. 6:7). That which is to be written on the heart and taught to the children is moral and spiritual truth about God, and love for God. *"Diligent"* means persevering and careful in work, involving steady, painstaking effort. We cannot be satisfied with reading Bible stories out of some book — no matter how good — to our children. We *must* put aside time for formal instruction if they are to grow to be mature Christians. This "formal instruction" should be both in the home and in the church!

(3) Informal teaching is also essential. "And shall talk of them when you sit in your house and when you walk by the way and when you lie down and when you rise up" (6:7). Could God have made it any more inclusive, conclusive, or clearer? We should by *word* and *example* talk of spiritual things to our children at home early in the morning, before and as we rest; when we are traveling; at all times. Speaking about Christian things should be as commonplace in our family relationships as is speaking about school, sports, or even the weather. After all, our whole lives are motivated by our love for God!

(4) If Christian parents so teach, it will result in a marked change in the character of the whole family. This is what the process of Christian maturity is all about. "And you shall bind them as a sign on your hand and they shall be as frontals on your forehead" (6:8). The truth of God and our love for God will affect what we *do* (be bound on your hands) and what we *think* and *say* (be as frontals, i.e., of/in/on, or at the front of our minds).

(5) Even our use of material possessions, given to us by God in the first place, will be as if we have written God's teachings on the doorposts of our house and on our gates (6:9). Not only will our lives and the lives of our children be transformed, but even our material things will be used so as to indicate that we have stamped God's will on them. The

Serving Christ: A Family Affair

direct result of applying God's plan for the family given by Moses will be *joint* ministry. (See also Deut. 11:18-21)

Ephesians 5:22-33; 6:1-4

This passage is all about family relationships.[8] Certainly, people view these verses differently. Some want to interpret them only from their particular family and cultural background. Some want to make them "contentious" and divisive to justify a certain perspective in the "war of the sexes" or the war going on in so many families — even many claiming to be Christian. Some simply ignore them. But it is our belief that these verses are intended to help us understand the beauty; responsibility; and, yes; the mystique of marriage and family; not to divide it, or structure it into a military hierarchy, or an "armed camp." Such interpretations simply ignore or misunderstand Ephesians and other passages that bear on Christian living in general.

(1) Paul tells us, "Wives, be subject to your own husbands, as to the Lord" (verse 22, also 23-24). Then, he goes on to draw a clear analogy (parallel, likeness, similarity) between husband and wife and Christ and His church. No matter how you may have heard or seen this passage interpreted, one thing is certain: Jesus *never* abused, belittled, beat or in any way mistreated His church! In fact, the image of Jesus is that of suffering servant (not tyrant), a relationship which is permeated throughout with love! This passage does not justify one spouse feeling superior to or mistreating the other. Verse 25 paints the picture of the husband sacrificing himself for his wife as Christ did for the church.

Remember the "context." Paul understood the difference that Jesus had made to the status of women. He

---

[8]Colossians 3:18-4:1 is a sort of parallel passage. See also 1 Peter 3:1,7.

knew (indeed, wrote) Galatians 3:28, "There is *neither* (*The New English Bible* says, "no such thing as") Jew and Greek, there is neither slave nor free man, there is neither male nor female; for you are all *one* (NEB, "one person") in Christ Jesus." There are also more than signs that Paul saw that in marriage husband and wife are equal partners who complement each other; e.g., 1 Corinthians 11:11, "And yet in Christ's fellowship woman is as essential to man as man to woman" (NEB). Verse 12 reads, "For as the woman originates from the man, so also the man *has his birth* through the woman; and all things originate from God."

(2) "Husbands, love your wives, just as Christ also loved the church and gave Himself up for her" (verse 25). Here, again, the message is strong and clear. The husband's love should be based on the pattern of the self-giving, self-sacrificing love of Jesus. We are reminded of Martin Luther's incisive statement, "To get a wife is easy enough, but to love her with constancy is difficult, and he who can do that may well be grateful to our Lord God."[9] Amen!

"The believing community is here compared to a maiden for whom Christ laid down his life that she might become his bride."[10] This same self-sacrificing love should be true of a husband's love for his wife. Speaking to husbands, John Wesley said, "The person in your house that claims your first and nearest attention, is, undoubtedly, your wife; seeing you are to love her, even as Christ loved the Church. . . ."[11]

---

[9]Luther, *Conversations with Luther*, Translated and edited by Preserved Smith & H. P. Gallinger (Boston: The Pilgrim Press, 1915), p. 63.

[10]F.F. Bruce, *The Epistles to the Colossians to Philemon and to the Ephesians*, in *The New International Commentary on the New Testament* (Grand Rapids: Eerdmans, 1984), p. 386.

[11]Wesley, *Sermons*, "On Family Religion," (1788), II, 1-2; in Thomas Jackson, Editor, *The Works of the Rev. John Wesley, A.M.*, Vol. VII, pp. 78-79.

Serving Christ: A Family Affair

(3) The image of verse 28 is again very powerful, "So husbands ought also to love their own wives as their own bodies. He who loves his own wife loves himself. . . ." First, the appeal to husbands to love their wives is based on the love of Jesus for His church. Now a further reason is given. Just as a man has a deep-rooted instinct to protect and care for himself, so a man should love his wife as if she were his own body! We cannot help but again recall Genesis 2:24 (which is indeed quoted in 5:31, just a few words below). "Since husband and wife are 'one flesh' or one body, to love one's wife is not merely a matter of loving someone else *as* oneself; it is in effect loving oneself. Adam recognized Eve as 'bone of my bones and flesh of my flesh' (Gen. 2:23); to love her therefore was to love part of himself."[12] Marriage is meant to be a "partnership" — in the strongest possible sense, where "two" become *one flesh* — entered into freely and with mutual consent for a lifetime.

We have often seen this passage abused! During a heated verbal disagreement between Christian husband and wife, this Ephesians passage is not infrequently "applied" / "invoked" this way.

Husband to wife: "You're supposed to obey me!"
   pointing an all too ready finger.
Wife to Husband: "You're supposed to love me!"
Husband: "I will — when you obey me first!"
Wife: "I will when you show me you love me!"

And, the "fight" goes on! Again, we must remember that Scripture must be taken in context — the context of a particular chapter and book, as well as in that of the whole of Scripture.

This passage and similar passages are often interpreted as if Paul was giving and reinforcing *positive role relationships*; that is: the husband is "lord and master," head of

---

[12]*Ibid.*, p. 391.

The Family in the Bible

the household; and the wife's obligation is "simply to obey." But this is not at all what Paul intended. There is another way of looking at this passage that makes sense and takes the Bible seriously.

Paul was not intending to give or reinforce positive role relationships at all, but just the opposite. You ask, "What do you mean 'just the opposite'?" Well, what if Paul was really saying:

> Husbands, you grew up in a world in which you were taught almost from infancy to "obey." Obedience is ingrained in you, almost as second nature. You don't have any problem with obedience. Husband, you on the other hand, need to learn a little more patience and compassion. You need to learn to express your love more freely!
>
> Wife, you grew up in a world in which you were taught almost from the beginning to "love." Love is ingrained in you. You don't have any problem with love. Wife, you need to learn a little more submission.

Maybe Paul was trying to supplement "negatives," or at the very least "weaknesses" in how the culture usually raised (and to a large extent still raises) boys and girls. Maybe at least part of what he was trying to say was that because of the very nature of how males are raised they need to be taught to be more gentle, compassionate — to love. And, that females, who are taught to be gentle and to love, need to be taught in the marriage relationship to also be submissive.[13]

---

[13]You say, "Boy, that interpretation is a stretch!" Not nearly as much of one as you may think. In fact, I (Terry) would argue that it makes much more sense in the total context of Scripture than the husband as "Lord and Master" one does. We have heard both very "conservative" and very "liberal" Christians stretch/interpret a Bible passage in a way that involved rather obvious "contortions" to get it to fit in with the "case they had built" to justify their views on a particular matter.

Serving Christ: A Family Affair

This as a *possible* interpretation[14] especially in light of Scriptures (some of which we have mentioned) which indicate equality between males and females. For example, wives are also told to love their husbands and both husbands and wives are told that their bodies belong to their mates, etc.

> The man should give his wife all that is her right as a married woman and the wife should do the same for her husband; for a girl who marries no longer has full right to her own body, for her husband then has rights to it, too; and the same way the husband no longer has full right to his own body, for it belongs also to his wife so do not refuse these rights to each other (1 Corinthians 7:3-5a, The Living Bible).

Regardless of how you may want to "interpret" this passages, it is clear that a loving husband sacrifices for his beloved wife; and equally clear that a loving wife sacrifices for her beloved husband; that the two become one flesh; and that they share in love and responsibility in raising a Christian family.[15]

(4) Certainly, children — not "adults"[16] — are to "obey

---

[14] Remember: the Bible is not self-interpreting! Not very often does someone in the Bible make a statement and then say, "now this is what I meant by that." Also, one doesn't just put a Bible under one's head overnight and know what it says, or means, the next morning. Nor do we necessarily know what the Bible says just because we grew up in a Christian home. Remember, too, that as good as some "study Bibles" are, the notes are not the "word of God."

[15] An interesting note: In most of the ultraconservative families we have known, where the man took a "hard line" in interpreting the wife's role as subservient, it was the wife who was the one who was expected to almost single-handedly raise the couple's children *and* often she — not he — paid the bills, balanced the checkbook and in effect controlled the family finances! We have always been rather "amused" at and confused by this.

[16] Who are adults? The age of 21 has been used for at least 143 years as a standard of manhood. "For as a young man arrived at the legal age of manhood is permitted thenceforth to manage his own affairs . . .."

your parents in the Lord, for this is right (Eph. 6:1).[17] Many people who write commentaries on Ephesians say that the respect of children for their parents is the very basis of the family and of family life. But even though some commentators think the phrase "'in the Lord' is of doubtful authenticity," we think it is most clear that, "It is in any case a Christian household that is envisaged...."[18] The context is a Christian home where the parents love and respect their children.

Here, too, is a passage that is often grossly misused. One famous parachurch ministry to teenagers, single people, and families seems to forget this obvious context of Christian parents. This ministry teaches that children should always obey their parents no matter how old they are, no matter whether the "children" are married or not, or even if the parents are not Christians. First, the Bible does not teach that parent/child is "the" eternal relationship. It teaches that a parent's responsibility, indeed the parent's greatest glory or joy, should be to see the child become a brother or sister in Christ, an equal in the Lord. Second, it ignores the fact that when children marry they are to leave father and mother and become one flesh. (Gen. 2:24, Matt. 19:5 and Eph. 5:31) This new family is in no way under the authority or control of their parents, nor is it meant to be!

Alexander Campbell, *The Millennial Harbinger* [MH] (1849), p. 37; and "Our laws and our taste have enacted, that we are men at twenty-one. Some, however, are nearer majority at eighteen, than others at twenty-five, and others are minors all their lives. *MH* (1850), p. 423; and "Our best Lexicographers concur in representing majority as the period of "full age" — the age at which our ancestors, in Britain and America, legally permit a young man to manage his own affairs, or to become his own guide and guardian in matters of property." Campbell, *MH* (1858), p. 421. Obviously, to us at least, this applies equally to men and women!

[17]See Chapter 5.
[18]F.F. Bruce, *Ibid.*, p. 397.

Serving Christ: A Family Affair

(5) "Honor your father and mother" (verse 2). The Ten Commandments are still important for Christians. The fifth is quoted here (See: Exod. 20:12 and Deut. 5:16). Again, we must see the context. The Scripture is talking about Christian children honoring their believing parents. Why wouldn't they want to honor them? We were overjoyed, incredibly honored recently when our son and his new "completer" — our new daughter — told us they want to model their family on ours. Could Christian parents be more honored? We couldn't be! But again, it is in no way saying that we are under the authority of our parents after we become independent legal adults or after we marry, when two become one body — one flesh — in Christ, a new family unit.

(6) "And, fathers do not provoke your children to anger; but bring them up in the discipline and instruction of the Lord" (verse 4).[19] As Locke said, "He that will have his son have a respect for him and his orders, must himself have a great reverence for his son."[20] Parents must be understanding. As Wesley said:

> Next to your wife are your children; immortal spirits whom God hath, for a time, entrusted to your care, that you may train them up in all holiness, and fit them for the enjoyment of God in eternity. This is a glorious and important trust; seeing one soul is of more value than all the world beside.[21]

What more "glorious and important trust" could there be than to put "immortal spirits" in our care? If a husband is

---

[19]See Chapter 5.

[20]Locke, *Some Thoughts On Education* (1693), Sec. 65. The critical edition is: *Some Thoughts On Education* Edited with an Introduction, Notes and Critical Apparatus by John W. and Jean S. Yolton (Oxford: Clarendon Press, 1989).

[21]Wesley, *Sermons*, "On Family Religion," II, 1-2; III, 18; in Jackson, *The Works of the Rev. John Wesley, A.M.*, Vol. VII, pp. 78-79, 85.

not to be a tyrant over wife, certainly husband and wife are not to be tyrants over their children. Discipline is essential! Discipline and punishment are different; punishment may at times be necessary, but neither should cause resentment. Neither should give the children the impression that they cannot do anything right.

Here, in this passage, we see a key to making serving Christ a family affair! Children *must* be helped to understand the significance of Jesus and His revelation to us. They should see in us a model of the personality *and* character of Him! While the church may help, this is the *parents'* responsibility — to be teachers, to be examples to their children. When we correct our children it should have the positive aim of developing qualities worthy of Him.

Therefore, discipline or punishment must be done in a Christlike attitude — with His love, compassion, tenderness, or gentleness. Responding to a child's misbehavior by getting angry ourselves and beating them is hardly a Christlike attitude! It is important to bear in mind: Children repeat what they hear, see, and experience — often later in life with their own children. "No man's knowledge here can go beyond his experience," said Locke.[22]

---

[22]Locke, *Essays Concerning Human Experience*, Book II, Ch. 1, Sec. 19.

CHAPTER THREE
What Makes a Home Christian?

A "family" is "an ecologically balanced environment for the growth of human beings, a shelter in the time of storm, an economic unit, a creativity center, a perpetual relay of truth, a museum of memories, an educational control, a formation center for human relationships, [and] an open door — with hinges and a lock."[1] We will say a bit more about what a "family" is in chapters 10, "The Family Today" and 11, "The Family and Ministry." Here our task is to discuss what makes a family or home distinctively "Christian."[2]

"What makes a home Christian?" is an interesting and important query. There is no question that the Christian family is — or should be — different from the non-Christian family. But is the difference one of "style" or one of "content"? Both! Many "Christians" do not know how to live the Christian life because they have only a minimal understanding of their faith. They try to live their entire lives on the first grade level. They never engage in disciplined study or service. You simply cannot become a mature Christian by accident. In order to grow YOU must discipline your life in study, prayer, worship, fellowship, and service.

---

[1]Edith Schaeffer, "What Is a Family?" in *Living & Growing Together: The Christian Family Today*, Edited by Gary R. Collins (Waco, TX: Word Books, 1976), pp. 11-23.

[2]You might find some helpful thoughts in: Jay E. Adams, *Christian Living in the Home* (Nutley, NJ: Presbyterian and Reformed Publishing Co., 1972). Olive J. Alexander, *Developing Spiritually Sensitive Children* (Minneapolis: Bethany House, 1980).

Serving Christ: A Family Affair

But before we start to discuss what a Christian home really is, we need to say a word or two about what it is *not*. Most homes make no pretense to be Christian; and in our unfortunate experience many which say they are, or think they are, need to think again! A home is not "Christian" in any real sense if: (1) The parents *say* they believe but *never* talk to each other about what that means in their lives or their children's lives. (2) They are only casual church members, only casually attend services, and don't really participate in the life of a believing fellowship. (3) They attend church every Sunday, but their "belief system" does not permeate their actions, attitudes, character, nurture, or relationships. (4) They never, or almost never, talk about or teach to their children what they believe, why they believe it, and why it is important to daily life and the future.

Further, (5) the parents are fine upright moral people respected in the community, but are not actively seeking to be transformed or to transform their family by embodying the teachings and Spirit of Jesus. Christians *should be* "moral," "upright," "respected"; but this alone does not make a person or a home Christian. We really must ask ourselves, "To whom or what are we committed?" Unfortunately, many people in the church today are committed to the church as an institution, but not to Christ as Savior and Lord. You can be committed to the church without being committed to Christ, but you cannot be committed to Christ without being committed to the church.[3]

So what makes a home Christian? Clearly, the opposite of the characteristics of a "non-Christian" home listed above would at least point in a positive direction. The rather obvious simple answer is as follows. A home is

---

[3]Some of these statements may seem a bit harsh, but think about them for a minute or two and we believe you will see the point.

What Makes a Home Christian?

Christian when both parents: (1) have accepted Jesus as Savior and Lord, (2) are professing believers who exemplify the character of Christ in relationship with each other and their children, (3) provide for the family an atmosphere of nurture and love permeated with the teachings of Jesus, (4) are continually trying to mature in their understanding and in living out their faith and (5) are sharing their faith, love, and abundance with others outside their immediate family.[4]

Basically a Christian family is one which has taken a stand for the Lord (1 above), lives a certain way (2) and by so doing, creates a special environment (3), which is always in the process of maturing (4), and shares (5) what they have with others. Let's look at each of these in turn.

The Christian Family has Taken a Stand

While driving home after an evening class when in graduate school, Terry remembers vividly hearing this "thought for the day" (a regular feature on a Chicago radio station), "Think about it: If you don't practice it, you don't believe it." Or, in today's' vernacular, "If you're gonna talk the talk, you gotta walk the walk." Rings true, doesn't it? Christianity is not a way of life, it is *life*. If you are not a Christian, you are not living, you are only existing. Conversely, if you claim to be a Christian and you are only existing; then, this should be your first clue that something is terribly wrong in your life! We do not think a person can truly be "in Christ" unless that person has a burning desire to change himself or herself, and then the world, toward the Christian ideal.

A home is Christian when *both parents have accepted Jesus as Savior and Lord*. It would seem that this ought to

---

[4]Though the biblical model for the family unquestionably includes two parents, of course, we understand that not every Christian family in this world is so constituted.

be intuitively obvious to anyone who had taken the time and energy to respond to an invitation to become a Christian. But amazingly, there are large numbers in every church who don't seem to really comprehend what it means to "accept Jesus as *Savior* or *Lord*." Week after week, year after year, we see parents come forward to accept Christ, or to transfer membership, or to dedicate themselves to raising their children as Christians; and then see in many *absolutely no visible* indication anything has changed. Often it is some time before they even come to church again.

What has failed? At the very least — evidently — somehow the church hasn't communicated what becoming a Christian, or being a Christian, or raising children as Christians, really involves. Perhaps, we shouldn't accept the confessions, transfers of membership, or parent dedications without being more certain that those making the petition really understand the request. Certainly, the church leadership needs to *communicate* the meaning of being a Christian more carefully, to *follow up* more diligently, and to *shepherd* more effectively.

What is it to have "faith"? "Faith is a conscious mental desire to do the will of the God of Scripture."[5] The concept of "faith" is the most central, foundational doctrine of all of Christianity, and yet the most misunderstood. Faith is not blindness, ignorance, or simple-mindedness.[6] A Greek dictionary will give you two essential aspects that penetrate to the heart of the biblical teaching: (1) trust or acceptance; belief that Jesus is God incarnate (embodied), with acknowledgment of His resurrection; and, (2) intellectual content, the revealed truth that is firmly believed, and is reflected in the life of the believer. The first part is involved in accepting Jesus as

---

[5] Miethe, *Reflections,* Volume One.
[6] The word "faith" appears 307 times in the New Testament.

What Makes a Home Christian?

Savior; the second, in living for Him as Lord!

Saving faith literally means to "believe into." It indicates a faith which takes a person out of oneself and into Christ. This kind of faith carries an intellectual assent that ties itself with the strongest possible bonds to Jesus. It *is* trusting a person — Jesus, the Christ. Thus the two aspects of faith make it not a passing thing, but a continuing attitude of life.[7] Accepting Jesus as Savior is the first part.[8] We must trust or accept that Jesus is God. "In the deepest sense, the Bible identifies truth with the person of Jesus Christ, the God-man who came to earth to die for the sins of the World" (John 14:6).[9]

So first, Jesus must be our Savior. This means at the very least, we must truly accept His forgiveness for our sins.[10] And, this *must* be allowed to impact our daily lives. Sometimes — in fact, often — it is harder to accept that we have been truly forgiven, than it is to accept Christ's deity. Our memory of past failure and faults causes regret, self-reproach, remorse and a haunting fear of failure. There is a universal disease of humankind. Everyone has it to a greater or lesser degree: It is the lack of a good self-image — an inferiority complex. As Christians, we must come to grips with this and mature through it! This acceptance should — ultimately must — affect our self-image. In the Lord we can have not only victory over temptation, but companionship in trial, joy in this life,

---

[7]Miethe, *Living Your Faith*, Chapter 1, "What is Faith, Really?" pp. 21-31.

[8]We are not talking about the "plan of salvation," or how one goes about being saved, but here we are talking about the implications of having been saved, having accepted Jesus as Savior.

[9]John Warwick Montgomery, *Faith Founded on Fact: Essays in Evidential Apologetics* (Nashville: Thomas Nelson, 1978), pp. 35-38.

[10]Remember Joe Stamey's most astute statement in note 25, p. 32 with regard to the fact that, ". . . our time which has almost lost any credible understanding of sin and — I'm afraid — even more of forgiveness."

Serving Christ: A Family Affair

and also, assured hope for the life to come.[11] But first, we must really accept that we are forgiven, and then we must live with that assurance.

The Christian Family Lives What They Believe

A home is Christian when both parents are *professing believers who exemplify the character of Christ in relationship with each other and their children*. This leads to the important fact that, as we have indicated, we must not only accept Jesus as Savior, but also as Lord. To accept Jesus as Lord means we must not only be willing to be "transformed," but actively seek it. God created us in His image, free beings.[12] In our hands we hold our destiny. To fulfill our destiny, to accomplish our dreams, there are three vices we must conquer: ignorance, laziness, and cowardice. These alone prevent us, God's heirs, from doing and being what we would dream to do and be!

We must be trying to live for Him, as He would have us live. This is an active ongoing daily process of commitment, or lifestyle and self-image changes. This process of making Jesus Lord of our lives really is lifelong. Here studying the Bible, the fellowship and teaching of the church, other Christians, other members of our family, reading good Christian books, etc. are important helps.

It is very important to develop "spiritual" discipline/s. Some important disciplines Christians should develop are: solitude and silence, prayer, simple and sacrificial living, meditation upon God's word and ways, and service to others. These are at the heart of the gospel. "We can increasingly resemble Christ in character and in power by *following him in his overall style of life*."[13] We

---

[11]Miethe, *Living Your Faith*, pp. 94-95.

[12]Ibid., pp. 41-54.

[13]See Dallas Willard, *The Spirit of the Disciplines: Understanding How God Changes Lives* (San Francisco: Harper & Row, 1988).

What Makes a Home Christian?

would do very well to heed what Paul writes: ". . . discipline yourself for the purpose of godliness; for bodily discipline is only of little profit, but godliness is profitable for all things, since it holds promise for the present life and also for the life to come" (1 Tim. 4:7-8).

Ideally, the time to develop good "spiritual" habits is when you are new in Christ.[14] It is much easier to practice good habits from the beginning. Parents, you have the glorious opportunity to help instill spiritual disciplines in your children while they are young when it is easier for them! Changing bad patterns developed over years is hard. May we suggest the following for your consideration. Great people of the faith have found these helpful throughout history.

(1) Begin and end every day with prayer. Prayer is basically a conversation with God. Remember, you can talk to God anytime you want!

(2) Read and meditate on a Bible passage daily — usually no more than a verse or paragraph. We suggest in the beginning from the New Testament.

(3) Never miss church worship unless absolutely necessary.

(4) Set aside a time each day for solitude; i.e., private prayer or meditation.

(5) Try in some way, by example or word, to share your faith in Christ Jesus daily.

---

[14]Thomas R. Kelly, *A Testament of Devotion*. Great Devotional Classics. Arranged and edited by Douglas V. Steere. (Nashville: The Upper Room, 1955). Elton Trueblood has many good things to say about this in *Alternative to Futility* (New York: Harper & Brothers Publishers, 1948). Trueblood's other books; e.g., *Company of the Committed, The Yoke of Christ, Confronting Christ, The Life We Prize, The Incendiary Fellowship*; are also helpful.

Serving Christ: A Family Affair

The Christian Family Builds a Habitat[15]

A home is Christian when both parents *provide for the family an atmosphere of nurture and love permeated with the teachings of Jesus*. Jesus must be Lord of each individual believer's life, and then He will be Lord of the family. When Jesus is Lord of the family one of the most important — essential really — priorities of the entire family will be to build a Christian environment in which to be nestled and nurtured. What makes a "home" a home and not just a "house"? The walls of a dwelling can reflect — and often do even when we are not aware they are doing so — the values of the family that living within. But far more important is the psychological atmosphere which is created and sustained within those walls.

Believe it or not, even the way we decorate our home can add to or take away from our awareness of Jesus. Deuteronomy 6 talks about writing your beliefs ". . . on the doorposts of your house and on your gates." Throughout history, Christianity has relied on symbols to help the believers see and understand the faith.[16] A symbol can express truth more simply and more profoundly than mere words — that's what makes it a symbol. Christian symbols can be "spiritual windows" through which God's truth can shine *if* people know, understand, or are reminded of the truth represented by the symbol. Symbols

---

[15]"Habitat" is a type of environment in which an organism normally lives. The place where a person is most likely to be found.

[16]A "symbol" is "1. Something that represents something else by association, resemblance, or convention; especially, a material object used to represent something invisible. 2. A printed or written sign used to represent an operation, element, quality, or relation, as in mathematics or music. . . . Latin *Symbolum*, sign, token, form Greek *sumbolon*, token for identification (by comparing with its counterpart), from *Sumballein*, to throw together, compare." *The New Ameriacn Heritage Dictionary of the English Language.* New College Edition. (Boston: Houghton Mifflin Co., 1976), p. 1302.

What Makes a Home Christian?

like the sign of the fish, the cross, a lamb, the Alpha and Omega, three intertwined circles (the Trinity), and a nativity scene relate powerful truths of the faith. Also, "symbols" are only important if they help remind us of who we really are. Otherwise, the "symbol" is not a symbol at all and is useless.

Yes indeed, "outsiders" can tell much about us and our priorities from our living environment. This is a very often overlooked way to reinforce our values and priorities and to witness. Surroundings in the home can have a subtle, but tremendous impact upon the growing child. If we should build our church buildings with families in mind (as we will see in chapter 4, "The Family First in the Church"), why shouldn't we think of our homes in the same way?

Now, we are not trying to tell you how to decorate your home. But pictures, wall hangings, plaques, etc. can surround us with, and remind us of, spiritual messages. For years, we had a plaque in our home with the words, "Therefore, my beloved brethren, be steadfast, immovable, always abounding in the work of the Lord, knowing that your toil is not in vain in the Lord" (1 Cor. 15:58). What more comforting words could there be to surround yourself with? Currently, the entryway of our home displays Isaiah 26:3, Micah 6:8, and Romans 8:37 in calligraphy. What better way to decorate your home than with Scripture![17]

The Christian Family Matures

A home is Christian when both parents are *continually trying to mature in their understanding and in living out their faith*. Christian maturity involves growing in the spiritual

---

[17]Beverly always has a calligraphy copy of Philippians 4:4-9 on the wall of her school classroom.

Serving Christ: A Family Affair

disciplines mentioned above, but especially involves a serious attempt to grow in prayer[18] and in the study of Jesus and the Scripture. Now, we are not at all against public education or educational classes in the church. In fact, we believe firmly in both! But one of the biggest mistakes Christian parents can make is to abdicate, to surrender, their right and responsibility to teach their children generally, and in the Lord, to others — either formally as in school or informally as by peer pressure. This is not only wrong; it can be fatal to the family![19]

The parent's most *basic* responsibility is the spiritual training of the child. We can draw from Paul's letter to Timothy that Timothy's *grandparents*[20] and parents were responsible for his early training in the Word. "For I am mindful of the sincere faith within you, which first dwelt in your grandmother Lois, and your mother Eunice, and I am sure that it is in you as well" (2 Tim. 1:5) and "that from childhood you have known the sacred writings which are able to give you the wisdom that leads to salvation through faith which is in Christ Jesus" (3:15). Further, the practice of teaching biblical principles is frequently specified to be in the home (1 Tim. 5:4,8).

A Christian family should set aside real, serious, precious time on a regular basis not just for family devotions,[21] but *for actual family education* as well. We are amazed at the amount of time the average family spends watching television when time could be spent so much

---

[18]More on this in chapter 9, "The Family that Prays and Plays Together."

[19]See D. Bruce Lockerbie, *Who Educated Your Child?* (Garden City, NY: Doubleday, 1980). Susan Schaeffer Macaulay, *For the Children's Sake: Foundations of Education for Home and School* (Westchester, IL: Crossway Books, 1984).

[20]Well over 3,300,000 children are actually now being raised by their grandparents according to NBC Nightly News, 26 March 1995.

[21]We will talk more specifically about this in later chapters.

What Makes a Home Christian?

more productively. Watching TV or playing games together really doesn't provide the depth of learning or nurture that is so much needed in a family.[22] And, it isn't just "families" in general who are suffering from this mistake; it is "Christian families" as well.

A woman, asking for advice, recently wrote:

> I have been so discouraged lately by the rudeness I see among my adolescent nieces, nephews and their friends. Why are they acting so differently than we did at their ages — not just to each other, but to adults? — Aunt Violet.

In our experience, the columnist's response, which we quote in part, was telling:

> There are many factors. *One is the behavior they see on television, where it's constantly implied that it's "cool" for both adults and kids to be rude and vulgar.* Even if your children are not allowed to see such TV shows, most of their friends do, and they want to be like their friends. The best most parents can do is monitor television, tell kids what they approve or disapprove and why, and not allow rude language by children's friends when they are guests in their homes.
>
> *Many parents seem too busy these days to take the time to tell children they will not allow rude language and behavior* or, even more important, to tell children what behavior or language they DO want and WHY they want it.
>
> This role takes lots more effort and time than it does to be a child's pal . . . [emphasis added].[23]

---

[22]You might want to see William L. Coleman, *Making TV Work for Your Family* (Minneapolis: Bethany House, 1983).

[23]Evelyn Petersen, "Teens nowadays have no sense of respect" in the syndicated column "Parents," *City Tab* (Abilene, Texas, Wednesday, Sept. 28, 1994), p. 5.

Something is terribly wrong with a family if the parents are too busy even to take the time to tell their children they will not allow rude language and behavior.

Herein rests part of the problem. Just "telling" children is not enough. We would argue that the proper way to treat others — or to instill behavior — is not just a matter of "words," but of *living*. Children learn this by the example we set within our family (as well as from without). Even with the pressure TV does undoubtedly exert directly and indirectly (through its effect on society as a whole), it should be clear that it is *not* "cool" to be rude and vulgar not just because parents say so, but because children know such behavior is totally against the values of the family.

Of course, Christian parents can do far more than this! When we accept the responsibility to bring children into this world, we say to God and to our society that *we are willing to take responsibility to nurture these children in every possible way so they will become mature, responsible, contributing Christian adults themselves*. Now, let's assume that you weren't taught all that well yourself. You have a chance to change this! This fact doesn't remove your responsibility to seek help and to expend serious time and energy learning so *you* can teach *your children* the values which must come from an understanding of your faith.[24]

The Christian Family Shares

The marking of the Christian is not in having a family, or in believing in one's family; but in honoring Christ by establishing and by being part of a particular kind of

---

[24]See Charlie Shedd, *You can be a Great Parent!* (Waco, TX: Word Books, 1982) and Joy Wilt, *An Uncomplicated Guide to Becoming a Super-Parent** (Word Books, 1980). Wilt defines a "super-parent" as "A normal human being who knows how to behave so that both parent and child live happy, fulfilled lives."

What Makes a Home Christian?

family. A family is Christian when it *shares faith, love, and abundance with others outside the immediate home.* One of the most basic marks of a Christian family is if family time and money are used to support their beliefs! Using such important family resources as time and money for God will impress the importance of their faith on the children as well. "Christian stewards" are people who realize that everything they have and all that they are, every aspect of their being, is a gift given to them by God to be used for Him.

It will be fairly easy to see, if we are truly trying to live for Christ. More and more our thoughts, time and energy, our personal and financial resources will be used for Him and His church. As our commitment matures, we will see a continually greater part of who we are in Christ and the Christian community. But bear in mind, this must be done within the context and nurture of the family. "Christian commitment" should not be used as an excuse for ignoring or not being responsible to the family!

Part of being in Christ is that you can be used without fear of being abused. This is easier stated than realized. Of course there will be people out there who will try to take advantage of you and your family. There is a fine line between waiting to become a "victim" and being "vulnerable" in the Lord. This is one of the many areas in which a strong believing community, a church, can be of great help to you. The existence of a loving, caring fellowship that really gives of itself, both to members and nonmembers, is one real test of whether a church is a real part of *the* church! Such a body can help you channel your giving to the best places and reduce the chance of your "being taken" or abused. It will also give you a most important support net of people with like minds (the mind of Christ), values, and commitments.

Chapter Four

The Family First in the Church

We begin this chapter by relating some very general thoughts about the church. The church has three grand tasks which are never complete and embody its very reason for existing: *Worship*, praising God in all aspects of life; *discipling*, teaching its own to mature in Christ; and *evangelism*, teaching others the good news of God's love. For the church to be the church, it must constantly be about: *restoration*, calling itself back to God's revealed will in Scripture; *reformation*, looking for a better, more efficient way to communicate the good news; and *revitalization*, producing new life from within and without. One word with three dimensions, "sharing" with God, "sharing" with each other in the body, and "sharing" with all humankind, expresses the threefold focus of the church in its mission.

Ministry is the glorious privilege and serious responsibility of *every* man, woman, and child who claims the name of Christ. Witnessing, loving, sharing themselves and their possessions, are essential ways ministry is expressed by individual Christians. Both the Old and New Testaments indicate the family is of first importance; therefore, it only makes sense that ministry would be carried on within the context of the family which is the oldest divine institution. The family existed before synagogues or churches and from God's viewpoint continues as the primary institution of love and learning.

As the family is the foundation of society, so it is the

Serving Christ: A Family Affair

very backbone of the church.[1] The church must not divide the Christian family and must teach the family how to minister and facilitate [to free from difficulties or obstacles; make easier, aid, assist] that ministry. And, yet, in our experience churches — granted, often unwittingly — do more to separate the family than to unite it or teach and encourage family ministry. But happily, many churches are now reevaluating their programs and purposes in light of the biblical emphasis on the home. It is time once again for the family to take its proper place in the purpose and function of the church. If this is to occur, it will not mean "business as usual," but will signal sweeping changes in the church today as most of us know it.

It should also be pointed out that many ministers would like to help in the recovery of the family, but are quite frustrated because it seems so difficult to make an impact on family life, in part, because the family unit is so often divided and in such disarray. If the family is not "divided" by the church, it is by the great number of organizations and events that clamor for attention so that the church is a faint din in the background. Then, too, an incredible percentage of modern day families are in such disorder themselves from the inside that they don't readily see the church as a place to go for help, or are ashamed to go. Some even resent the church when it tries to "interfere" with their family and attempt to give comfort and help. In many places the state of relation between churches and families has so disintegrated that hope for the future looks quite bleak.

Thus, while most ministers admit the importance of both home and church often they tend to disjoin the two and view them as separate entities because of what seems

---

[1] See Olaf R. Johnston, *Who Needs the Family?* (Downers Grove, IL: InterVarsity Press, 1979).

to be a practical necessity. Such a false schism was unknown in the days of the New Testament church. An examination of early church history tells us that there were no church buildings until almost the third century. Local congregations most often met in homes for worship and for their fellowship gatherings. In fact, fellowship is one of the New Testament patterns which relates to both home and church.

Such a separation ultimately has disastrous consequences for both home and church for the "church" is really the fellowship of families united to inform, strengthen, and inspire one another. There may be special cases where a church can exist without families, but it is hard to imagine the church surviving without families. This much is absolutely certain: God intended the family to be the basic unit of society and church. The very concept of "fellowship" and "family" are taken from the single household and transposed to the church "family" (Colossians 3).[2]

Yet if the family is the backbone of the church, so too the church has a responsibility to help build and strengthen Christian homes. Ministers are beginning again to realize that *the home is truly the "laboratory" for both the practical application of, and the gauge for the effectiveness of, the teaching and preaching ministries of the church*. The real "success" of a church must be seen in its effectiveness in building and nurturing strong, vibrant families! This cannot be stressed too much. Further, in all fairness, we must admit that the scope of the church's responsibility today is staggering, but this is all the more reason why the place of the family within the church is so important to the future. So often in seemingly trying to do the work

---

[2]Kenneth Gangel, *The Family First: Biblical Answers to Family Problems* (Minneapolis: His International Service, 1972), pp. 128-129. Reissued rev. ed. (Winona Lake, IN: BMH Books, 1979).

Serving Christ: A Family Affair

of the family, the church is making toil for itself which is both unreal and unbiblical.

This building and nurturing of the family is not likely to happen by accident. It's not likely to happen except where strong family units already exist in a particular subculture. But this too is deceiving. Even then, the church must work hard and intentionally to keep the family strong and maturing with regard to the faith, but also in many other areas as well. We have seen numerous examples of communities that were built on strong families start to decay because the particular subculture, and the churches in it, took the "health" of the family for granted. These churches *thought* their families were strong in spite of clear signs to the contrary.

Thankfully, many churches are beginning again to see the vital importance of their Christian education programs to the church and to the family. "Rather than just Sunday school and Evangelistic services held together by a string of buses,"[3] some churches are beginning to deliberately construct programs for families, rather than programs that actually divide families — into age groups, etc. — as in the past. The church must listen to the needs and interests of the family, not just "pontificate" to individuals and families.

What Can the Church Do?

What can a church do to unite the family rather than at least potentially divide it? We must start by admitting that a problem exists. Then, and only then, will we start to look for solutions. "Band-Aid" solutions will no longer do! "Token emphases such as a yearly Family Week, a Family Night . . . or a [one] premarital counseling session before the wedding" will never unite the family and the

---

[3]Gangel, *The Family First*, p. 130.

The Family First in the Church

church, nor will such "develop strong Christian homes."[4]

We must get out of the "box"! We must stop thinking from within the strictures of a closed historical view — "this is the way it has always been done so it must be done this way" — which is an artificial constraint in the first place. Bottom line: We *must rethink every aspect of the church's existence and redirect and redeploy a major part of its effort and resources around the family*. This, too, cannot be overemphasized. If there was ever a time when we needed to go back to a thorough and mature understanding of Scripture; and at the same time to step out and be truly innovative in building programs, and even building churches themselves, today is that time.

We are not saying that the church should not be involved in caring for the poor, feeding the sick, sheltering the homeless; helping the "down and almost out" of society. Certainly, the church must be about this. This is one real gauge of whether the church is really the Church! But even these type ministries should be done, can be done, both with families in mind, *and carried out by families*. Families — parents and children — should work together as part of the church to feed the hungry, etc. Can you imagine a more effective learning situation, more effective way to give thanks, than taking our children with us when we serve or witness; or even bringing our "service" into our very homes so our children can see even this type of ministry as an important part of family life.

What, specifically can the church do? One does not have to wildly stretch one's imagination to see that perhaps the home could once again be given a place of centrality as it was in the first three centuries of the

---

[4]Julie Gorman, "Family Enrichment through the Church" in *Facing the Future: The Church and Family Together* edited by Gary R. Collins (Waco, TX: Word Books, 1976), p. 62.

existence of the church. Much of what is done in the church building can be effectively transferred back to the family. There are rather simple, as well as rather astounding, possibilities when you stop and think about it.

(1) The church should begin by consciously making one of the essential themes of its existence and self-identity the family. This is the way it should be. This is how God ordained it to be. Serious effort must be expended to be certain that this "essential theme" permeates every aspect of church life. We would suggest starting by appointing a task force empowered with a clear understanding of the importance and possible scope of the task ahead to seriously study the question and the possibilities. This group should include families, children, and leaders in the church.

(2) The preaching and teaching must be geared toward emphasizing the importance of the family and the home. This should begin as soon as possible. Of course, before significant change can occur, a significant percentage of the membership must be "on board." But there is no reason that a minister couldn't start with a monthly "family (emphasis) Sunday." During this service the sermon would be about some aspect of the family, home, or the relationship of the church to the home. Church members as individual families — as well as individual church members who are part of the "family of God"[5] — should have an important and active role in every aspect of the service.

(3) Divide the church into smaller family units and have these meet in homes for fellowship, teaching, prayer, worship, etc. One example: Plan a regular once a

---

[5]There are subtle — and not so subtle — ways to emphasize that every individual member of the church is highly valued and nothing being done should in any way make an individual member; i.e., who has no other biological family members in the church, feel left out or unwanted.

The Family First in the Church

month family evening in homes in place of Sunday night services (if you have them). It will take some planning and some regular work, but someone can be put in charge (as an aspect of their ministry) of dividing up the individuals and families of the church into, say, five units which will meet one Sunday night a month in the home of one of the five. Obviously, the individual families which make up these groups need to be rotated on a fairly regular basis so that the groups don't remain the same.[6]

(4) *Strengthen the Christian education program of the church at every level.* Far from making the education program of the church obsolete, this new emphasis on family demands that it be made as strong as possible! While the children's educational program is very important, having a strong "children's" program cannot be an excuse for overlooking or forgetting the adult program. The church must have a strong adult education program, for this is essential to strengthening the home. Ultimately, if your church does not have a strong adult education program, we believe that if you look carefully (deeply, not just on the surface) you will find that what you thought was a strong children's program wasn't so strong after all. In other words, you really cannot have a strong children's program if you don't have a strong adult program. Anything that can link the Sunday School with the home is worth exploring.

Even the organization of the Sunday School needs to be rethought. Some churches have actually adopted a "Sunday School Family Style" to replace the traditional approach. In one example:

> A single master-teacher launches the learning experience . . . with a short, five- to ten-minute introduction. Then the Sunday school is divided into two-

---

[6]One group can meet in the church if it is inconvenient for some to come together in a home.

Serving Christ: A Family Affair

> family groupings with mom, dad, and all children from four to eleven seen as a "family." Those children whose parents do not come are "adopted" into one of the families there. The parents and kids are given an 8½×11 sheet of paper on which are outlined six to eight different kinds of learning activities or studies. Each two family group selects from the list and moves on into its own learning experience. The learning activities are designed to encourage exploration of the Scriptures, sharing with others inner feelings and experience, and applying truths discovered to present needs. Near the end of the Sunday school time, the whole school reassembles, and one member of each two-family learning group shares a brief report.

The idea in Sunday School Family Style is to train parents by participation to share with their own children. Parents and children are viewed as learners together. The important aspect in this example is to help "the parents learn to *share* their faith rather than tell information."[7]

We agree, there is a danger that we will grasp at superficial solutions to the family's very basic needs. We are not sure that "program gimmicks" are the answer. Rather, what is important — whatever the plan followed — is that families experience a refreshing learning experience as a shared event. You would think that something so basic as parents "sharing" their faith with their own children should come naturally, but you would then be surprised at how many parents have asked us for help with this. It is often difficult, but well worth the effort, to open up lines of communication where there were none before; especially about something as personal as "faith." Opening up such communication is absolutely essential if the family is to become what the Bible intends it to be and if we are

---

[7]Larry Richards, "How the Church Can Help the Family Face the Future" in Collins, editor, *Facing the Future*, p. 19.

The Family First in the Church

going to affect the state of the family in our churches.

(5) Offer a regular evening class, small in size, for invited families only, which both teaches and models family evangelism and discipling. Families should include those with preschoolers and on up. If the class is begun with a meal, opportunity is given to model family fun times around the table, etc. Maybe the class will go for a year, but meet only once a month. Experiment. Again, the purpose of the class is to both teach and model evangelism techniques applied to the family as a unit and to help the family learn how to encourage and support individual members in evangelism and discipling.

(6) Offer classes (different levels of classes) on family life education, parenting, relationship building, seminars on the home, etc. regularly. These can be structured in many ways, and around different group needs. For example some seminars might be:
- "How to Pray with Your Wife,"
- "The Needs of the Young Mother,"
- "How to Build Self-Esteem in Your Children,"
- "Love as the Best Means for Discipline,"
- "Building a Workable Family Budget,"
- "How to Make Holidays Christ-centered,"
- "How to Use Your Home for God," etc.[8]

Develop classes/seminars that both *model* and *instruct* as they meet family needs.

Again and again over many years of teaching, Beverly has heard parents — often in tears — say, "We were never taught how to be parents and this is the one thing we needed most." Well, folks, guess who should be offering

---

[8] A "hidden" bonus: such classes will help not only the families in your church. We think that classes like these, properly done, should be widely advertised to the community at large because they can be tools for evangelism as well; i.e., why not "hook up" some of your young mothers with others in need of a loving, caring church!

Serving Christ: A Family Affair

such classes? THE CHURCH. These classes could be offered in the church and in homes. Home Bible study classes constructed around and geared for the family can be most helpful too and can incorporate some of the needed aspects of a "parenting" class.[9]

(7) Family outings, camping, church picnics planned and executed by the church are some possibilities.[10] Yes, even the "potluck supper" *can* be meaningful if done right.[11]

---

[9]You might find helpful: Paul R. Ackerman and Murry M. Kappelman, *Signals: What Your Child Is Really Telling You* (New York: Dial Press, 1978) which discusses the methods of nonverbal communication used by children, explains their meaning, and provides suggestions as to how the child's felt needs may be met. Gerald R. Adams and Thomas Gullotta, *Adolescent Life Experiences* (Monterey, CA: Brooks/Cole Publishing Co. 1983) which helps ministers and parents understand both the why and how of the life-changes through which our children pass. Ruth G. Boyer, *The Happy Adolescent* (Palo Alto, CA: R. and E. Research Associates, 1981). Barry & Patricia M. Bricklin, *Strong Family, Strong Child: The Art of Working Together to Develop a Healthy Child* (New York: Delacorte Press, 1970) who by combining their skills as psychologists and as parents, provide valuable counsel and practical guidelines for rearing strong, mature, emotionally healthy children. Dorothy C. Briggs, *Your Child's Self-Esteem: The Key to Life* (Garden City, NY: Doubleday, 1975) is a most important work even though the author's humanism is evident. Ross Campbell, *How to Really Love Your Teenager* (Wheaton, IL: Victor Books, 1981) is highly acclaimed. Richard D. Dobbins, *Venturing into a Child's World* (Old Tappan, NJ: Fleming H. Revell Co., 1985). Frances L. Ilg, Louis B Ames, & Sidney M. Baker, *Child Behavior*, Rev. ed. (New York: Harper & Row, 1981) is considered excellent by many. James A. & Mary Kenny, *Whole-Life Parenting* (New York: Continuum Publishers, 1984) is a vigorous challenge to build the kind of beliefs, values, and goals that will prepare your children for life. Helen Neville & Mona Halaby, *No-Fault Parenting* (New York: Facts on File Publications, 1984). Charles E. Schaefer, *How to Influence Children: A Complete Guide for Becoming a Better Parent* 2d ed.. Revised and expanded (New York: Van Nostrand Reinhold Co., 1982) is a classic in the field of childrearing.

[10]See Lloyd & Elsie Mattson, *Rediscover Your Family Outdoors* (Wheaton, IL: Victor Books, 1980).

[11]We need not over look the old — and maybe worn — activities of the past. In some areas mother-daughter, father-son, parent-teen events are popular. But these also need to be "rethought" with new vitality in mind.

The Family First in the Church

Think of fun ways the families of the church can be together as families, but again remember to structure most of the individual activities around the family unit. We know of churches which make the effort to have regular all-church picnics, and some that get together on a regular basis for the *families* to play baseball. Perhaps a member or two has some land which can be used on a regular basis for such activities. If you are in an inner city situation, rent (or try to encourage a facility exchange to offset the cost of renting) a place different from the church building for fun family activities. Perhaps a city park with a large number of adults to ensure supervision and security.

We know of churches in relatively small cities that have actually built rather elaborate "Family Fun Centers" with all sorts of games and activities available within. These churches usually make this facility available to other churches, schools, and to individuals at a small cost. Of course, "mega-churches" often have every kind of facility built into the church complex — from workout rooms, to bowling alleys, to saunas, etc.

But our advice here is to be very careful. The church must always be much more than a "social club" or a place for people to "get away" from the world. Building such elaborate facilities can end up with you caught in a "trap" that may actually mediate against or undo the desired effect! Bigger is not all at always "better," in fact, in our experience it rarely — if ever — is. It is certainly not more "spiritual." More is not always what is needed. On the other hand, an empty church doesn't glorify God either.

These are just some possibilities. There *is* time available! The family and the church can come back together. By age eighteen, most children have already watched over 20,000 hours of television. This is enough time to earn at least bachelor and master's degrees, perhaps even a

Serving Christ: A Family Affair

Ph.D.[12] Surely, much of that time could be put to better use for the family, and for Christ and the church!

We should never fear being creative! The "only" constraint in getting out of the "box" is we must be sure that what we are doing is consistent with biblical teaching and general Christian principles, morality, etc. Now is not the time to lessen our ties to Scripture or the historic truths and commitments of Christianity. THERE WILL NEVER BE SUCH A TIME! Also, we must be careful that a "neutral method" or application doesn't in the long run undermine the very result we are seeking; e.g., as has happened in some mega-churches, and "family fun centers."

The church that "thinks family" will develop increasingly creative methods for providing a treasure of family experiences. But someone is going to have to be responsible for implementing any program. In his administrative experience, Terry learned a long time ago that you do not have a program if someone is not in charge of it, if someone doesn't feel responsibility or a sense of "ownership" for it.

The church must not only illuminate by clear teaching on the home, but it must also admonish the family to positive action, give constant encouragement and support, and enrich the individual family by modeling what the family ought to be to one another within the broader body of Christ. This is the task! Whatever happens, do not become discouraged. It may take years of prayer, planning, and practice to accomplish the goal. But one thing is sure: Nothing will happen if we give up!

---

[12]If one figures a bachelor's at 136 *credit* hours, a master's another 30 credit hours, and a Ph.D. a further 30 (which is not uncommon today) and allowing one hour outside of class for every hour spent in class (it is doubtful in many cases it averages that many) you would have 2360 hours left over!

Revitalize Worship With the Family in Mind

Rethink our worship services! Is it really enough to have a "children's sermon" and then dismiss them to "children's church"? At least, must this *always* be the way it is done? Now, granted having a "children's sermon" if it is truly for the children (and as much or more effort goes into it as the adult sermon) is better than ignoring them altogether or never having them in the "adult" service. But all too often the children's sermon becomes a "cutesy" way of communicating with the adults at the expense of the children!

Is it really true that the best thing for the parents is to be "free" from their children during the worship service? We have heard the "arguments." Granted, some parents prefer not to have to "fight" their children during the service, and perhaps alternatives should be provided for them, but maybe — just maybe — if we structure our worship service to be family oriented — which means being willing to rethink every aspect of it — so that the family is emphasized and encouraged to participate, maybe even some of the "unruly" children will see their peers in the service and want to "behave" and be there as well. At any rate, "behavior" would be much less of an issue if the whole service was planned around and included the family.

There are many creative ways that the "worship service" can be restructured around the family. Think! Why should the service or even the sermon be structured with only the adults in mind? Why can't the minister modify the presentation so that different age levels are, in turn, spoken to and included in the same message. We *know* it will take time and effort, and growth on the part of the presenter! But are these "hurdles" so insurmountable that we don't try to improve for the sake of effective ministry?

Serving Christ: A Family Affair

Build New Church Buildings Around the Family

So many of our church buildings, even relatively new ones, were built to be "beautiful" buildings. But when you stop and view them with other than the eyes of the past — assumed to be the "appropriate" form for a church — and view them from the eyes of a small child or a family, we get a totally different perspective. Often, they do more to frighten and "alienate" than to bid WELCOME. We realize that every church can't just tear down its buildings and start new. But even the realization of what we are about to say could help us look at our existing physical plants with an eye to making them as "user friendly," family friendly as possible within the limits of possibility. In other words, we need to be really serious about making the physical environment more conducive to the family, and not let it be just some formal place with a "wooden" view of God and worship.

Future church buildings should be built with families in mind. We know a church that was constructed with an eye to versatility and family. The "altar," not very much higher than the main floor, is rounded and very accessible. The sides are sloped for wheelchair access. The entire floor — altar and main — is carpeted the same. None of the furniture is fixed in position; i.e., the pulpit and communion table are easily moved so the platform can be used in drama productions. The congregation sits on attractive wooden and padded fabric covered chairs which can be arranged in any pattern, or stacked for storage. The front of the sanctuary is simple but attractively designed with stone work, natural plants, a small waterfall, and light from above. Upon entering, a large part of the right side of the sanctuary is an open "parlor" with living room furniture and a glass exterior building wall, again with plenty of light and plants inside and outside, and a feeling of openness, comfort, and of home. The building is very tastefully designed and decorated, has maximum versatility, and looks like a place where a "family" would feel right at home. Why shouldn't a church look this way? It is a most inviting environment.

Implement Serious Pre-Marital Education

If we are really earnest about restoring the importance and place of the family in our community and in our church, we need to start when the family is in process of forming, before attitudes have been largely solidified and are hard to change. Churches need to get serious about real pre-marital *education* which needs to occur long before a wedding date is set. Ideally, this education needs to begin in the home by the parents at a rather early age. The church should have classes on premarital education starting at junior high school age.

What goes by the name of "premarital counseling" often amounts to very little, or nothing. The minister should not be obligated — nor feel "forced" because the church building is a beautiful place for weddings — to marry "everyone who comes along." It seems to us that performing marriages "indiscriminately" for non-church members, or even the offspring of members who are obviously not ready for marriage, just helps to propagate the problem we all decry — the high divorce rate and broken families!

The Church Must "Get Serious" About Education and Leadership

Another, rather "obvious" step would be for the church to get serious about adult education as indicated above. By far, most of the adult classes we have experienced are really a travesty on education. To change this situation, we must give church school teachers the time and resources necessary to prepare classes; as well as conduct effective ongoing teacher training classes. In one church we know, the leadership goes to the individual they think could teach a certain class and basically says, "If you are willing to take on this class, we will provide all the resources you need. We want you to take six months to prepare, and when you are ready we will schedule the class." Rather amazing when you realize that so many church classes — not to mention sermons — are prepared the night before.

Further, if we are to "get serious" about being a church in the first place — which is ultimately essential to helping the family — leadership must be considered. In many of the churches we have experienced there is almost no time or effort put into building leadership. *We desperately need to have strong leadership development programs*. Any organization, including the family and the church, is going to be all but "dead in the water" without good, effective leadership. Such leadership should not be given or taken on lightly! A church cannot grow without leadership.

The Church Needs to Rethink Evangelism

We need to place a new *emphasis* on evangelizing the family, *and* using the family as a tool for evangelism. For far too long we have gone after children or young people without really promoting the idea that Christ is for the *whole* family and He *wants* entire families. Again, often "success" or "failure" is conditioned by our conceptual understanding of what we are doing and the emphasis we bring to the task. We will not always succeed with the entire family, but it is our emphasis on the issue that needs to change. In fact, in a reverse sort of way, when the church targets individuals without attempting to involve the whole family in the process, the family unit can be "negatively" effected — an effect that hurts the new Christian as well as other family members.

The Church Must Not Be In Competition With the Home

"In face of the increasing numbers of people needed to 'run the church,' the ecclesiastical 'faithful' are so heavily involved in the church that their family relationships pay the price and their children are robbed of what is rightfully theirs."[13] It is not just the small struggling church that may not be putting the family first. Often it is the very church we think of as the "greatest success" which is "destroying" the family! We must not "church" people to death! We must not monopolize the parents in the name of the "work of the church." If we do we cheat them and their children of the very Christianity *within the family* those very parents are working so hard to implement within the church.

All of this will be quite "tricky" and will take a lot of planning with regard to different areas and specific situations. But one thing is sure, the church can help avoid conflict with the home by establishing a program which does not monopolize evening time. Part of the solution to this problem could be with creative programming before school. Children do all kinds of things they consider "important" before school these days. Or, perhaps, programs need to be planned in the early afternoon, or right after school in many cases.

Of course, we must seriously analyze just what "tasks" we are giving our people in the process of "running the

---

[13]Julie Gorman, "Family Enrichment through the Church" in Collins' *Facing the Future*, p. 61. In all fairness, Gorman also relates the other extreme: ". . . those individuals, convicted by their lack of family involvement in the past, who have become so family oriented that they decline to serve on church boards and who explain their absence form church gatherings as 'spending time with the family — which is biblical.'" Yet in our experience, we can't help but feel that in a majority of cases these parents may have an understandable claim, especially in light of the burnout rate in churches, and the lack of really "profitable" services.

Serving Christ: A Family Affair

church" to see if these are really important at all! Sometimes the worst possible scenario is actually being played out in the relationship between family and church. The following is a telling story (and terrible attitude):

> Some church bulletins read as though they were deliberately calculated to divide the family by making sure one member had to be present at the church every evening of the week. A pastor told me . . . he **deliberately** schedules church activities this way because, "They don't know what to do with themselves at home anyway. They just sit around and watch television."

What this minister "apparently failed to realize is that he has the strategic responsibility to teach families what to do at home."[14] It seems that this realization would constitute almost a "revelation" to some ministers.

Training the parents to be able to seriously "minister" to their children is an important part of the solution; for example, in holding "church" events structured for and around families in the home. We truly have a long way to go in this area of the family first in the church. Of the following, there can be no question. The Christian home is the most important organization for Christian nurture! The church is only properly carrying out its task when it focuses its ministries on families and enables, rather than hinders, the teaching activities of the parents.

If we accomplish nothing else, we hope that this book will (1) help individual families see how essential family ministry is; and (2) help individual churches see how needed serious change is today if we are to impact society and the family in the Twenty-first Century. There has never been more responsibility on the leadership of the local church. Individual congregations must be designed,

---

[14]Gangel, *The Family First*, p. 132.

The Family First in the Church

and in many, many cases redesigned, to affirm the importance of the family and to provide an environment in which lifestyle changing ministry can and does take place. This is the real hope for the family and for your future as a congregation! We must pray and pray and pray and also *take action.*

CHAPTER FIVE

The Family and Worship

The family *must* be matured into a "worshiping unit" both in the church and in the home. Of course, one needs to ask an essential question, "What is worship?" Terry addresses this subject more thoroughly in his book, *Following Jesus*, than is possible here. Basically *"worship is an attitude of life."* The New Testament never speaks of a "worship service" or of an "act of worship," or of "special places" in which to assemble to worship. It is not, nor should it be, confined to a specific building or place. *Worship is a feeling of adoration to God that expresses itself in a life of service.* Christian worship involves the whole life. Christian worship is to glorify God, it enables us to grow in grace, it helps us realize that presenting our lives is our offering to God (Rom. 12:1-2), and worship should help spread God's Presence (influence) in our world![1]

Worship is communion with God! "Worship" is an attitude of life because in its fullest, it must be the realization that we are always in God's presence, always under His Lordship, always alive by His power and His grace! Family worship is taking our family, our needs, our desires, our dreams, our thankfulness, our very lives before God and bringing God before and into our family. We must teach our children that living for God is as real and vibrant as life can get. It is life itself. What we are

---

[1]See Chapters 10, "The Meaning of Worship," 11, "The Nature of Worship," 12, "The Purpose of Worship," and 13, "The Attitude of Worship" in Miethe, *The New Christian's Guide to Following Jesus*, pp. 67-84.

Serving Christ: A Family Affair

trying to do in family worship is to help every member have a living encounter with God, not an occasional "close encounter" as if with some alien, but a warm continual growth as with a lover or friend.

Our task here is to discuss why the family should, and how it can, worship together effectively. Some parents determined to be "effective Christian parents" gather their children around the table after supper for a half hour of family worship. There they share in Bible reading, prayer, and an occasional hymn. Some readers might say, "This would be great — if we ever had supper together anymore." For some the idea of even doing this much — having a half hour for family worship — is felt to be beyond the realm of possibility.

Our lives are so hectic! But *who* sets or allows the schedule? Sure, the "path of least resistance" seems on the surface to be the easiest, but actually it is the hardest because we almost always reap negative results later. Any kind of discipline is hard, but is its own reward — and is well worth it. There is an old saying, "The only evidence of life is growth" to which we add "and growth always involves pain," or at least what is perceived as painful at the time. But discipline almost always turns out to be the source of real pleasure in the long run.

When it comes to ethics (or almost anything for that matter), *most of us are conditioned for short-term pleasure, not conditioned for long-term happiness*! A very wise man once said that everything in life has its season or "appointed time" (Eccl. 3:1-8). When we choose to practice anything in excess, we give up the freedom to do other, sometimes more important or more meaningful things; e.g., when we constantly practice the freedom to overeat and not exercise, we give up the freedom to be in good physical shape, or to be able to walk very far without losing our breath.

In relating the story of a family which spends a half

hour in family worship each evening after supper, the Gangels say, "Sounds good, doesn't it?" But then they tell us that the fifteen-year-old "resents missing his favorite television program," the twelve-year-old "complains that she can't spare the time from homework responsibilities," the seven-year-old is "uninterested and shows it by making noises and disturbing the others." As the children fuss more and more, the parents "force the issue. Some evenings family worship erupts in a verbal battle upsetting everyone for the next several hours!"[2]

Nice story? But the reality is that this family already has some serious problems of self-identity! Also, we believe that with the proper emphasis on love, who we are as a Christian family, and with proper understanding, such a half-hour exercise can be very rewarding. But it need not happen every night or just after dinner. Think! Be creative!

Biblical Basis

During the Reformation, one of the important biblical doctrines Martin Luther[3] rediscovered (it was clearly there all along in Scripture) was the "priesthood of all believers." That each individual Christian is a minister was also originally one of the linchpins of the Restoration Movement. But sadly, this has gone the way of history as well. In writing to believers in general, Peter says, "You are . . . a royal priesthood . . . that you may proclaim the

---

[2]Kenneth O. & Elizabeth Gangel, *Between Christian Parent and Child* (Grand Rapids: Baker, 1974), p. 59.

[3]Steven Ozment, *The Age of Reform, 1250-1550: An Intellectual and Religious History of Late Medieval and Reformation Europe* (New Haven, CT: Yale University Press, 1980) is a helpful book. With regard to Luther see John M. Todd, *Luther: A Life* (New York: Crossroad Publishing Co., 1982); Roland H. Bainton, *Here I Stand: A Life of Martin Luther* (New York: Mentor Books, 1950); and Vergilius Ferm, *Cross-Currents in the Personality of Martin Luther* (North Quincy, MA: The Christopher Publishing House, 1972).

Serving Christ: A Family Affair

excellencies of Him who has called you out of darkness into His marvelous light" (1 Pet. 2:9).[4] The tradition of priesthood provided for a ministry of the priest to himself (Lev. 9:7). Unquestionably, a "priest" has a duty to minister to others, but surely, this "royal priesthood" must begin in and with the family! Christenson rightly calls parents "priests of the Lord! Called and ordained by God as priests unto their children."[5] Amen!

"Some people think that the Bible contains many passages on the importance and technique of family worship. Actually it does not." There is really nothing *per se* regarding "technique" as such. But the "general tone" of the Bible more than "implies that the home is the central source of spiritual teaching."[6] Remember our material on Deuteronomy 6:4-6 in chapter two.

The fact that the Bible doesn't say much about technique doesn't lessen its importance, or mean that family worship is not important. It does, however, give us the freedom to experiment with a form that best meets the needs of each individual family. *This freedom, though, doesn't reduce our responsibility as parents to teach our children what we believe, why we believe it, and how to practice it.* Obviously, the most effective way to teach anything is to do it in the most "natural" way as a normal part of daily life and by example. This is clearly the emphasis of the Deuteronomy passage. Yet saying this doesn't eliminate the need for formal instruction in the home!

Have you ever seen a family where one parent — or both — was "sold" on baseball, hockey, camping, or

---

[4] See also 1 Pet. 2:5; Rom. 12:1,2; 2 Cor. 5:17-20; Rev. 1:6; 5:10; 20:6; Eph. 4:11-12; and Miethe, "Ministry and the Christian," chapter 17 in *The New Christian's Guide to Following Jesus*, pp. 103-110.

[5] Larry Christenson, *The Christian Family* (Minneapolis: Bethany House Publishers, 1970), p. 157.

[6] Kenneth O. & Elizabeth Gangel, *Between Christian Parent and Child*, p. 60.

The Family and Worship

scouting? Surely. We have all seen parents use one of these interests to enrich the family; and, we have seen others get "fanatical" and as a result drive their children from them as well. But the "trick" is to do whatever we do in such a natural way that the children "catch" the enthusiasm and the activity becomes a time that enriches the lives involved. Surely, worship can and should be such a rich activity or time for Christian families.

Some General Principles[7]

Because each family is free to define for itself how "devotions" and/or "family worship" can best be carried out in the home, the possibilities are almost endless and can also be very exciting. Again, there is no substitute for *you* getting out of the "box" and *daring* to be original and innovative. And, if you come up with something that works well for your family please do share it with others in the church. It could well work for them too. Here are three very evident principles.

(1) *Flexibility*: We *need* to be flexible! Yes, it is important to establish "routines," but these should not be so rigid that they are unworkable, nor should we abandon them, or feel like they are failures, if we miss once in a while. Robert Richardson says of Alexander Campbell's family:

> Family worship was not allowed to become a mere routine. He [Alexander] knew well how to maintain its interest, by making it a means of real instruction and enjoyment; and, by encouraging familiar inquiry on the part of the young, he managed to bring forward and to impress indelibly the most charming practical lessons from the sacred writings, having

---

[7]We make no claim that these are unique to us. Most have been gleaned from one source or other over twenty-five years of marriage and even more of ministry.

> always something novel and agreeable to impart zest and interest to exercises which in many cases are apt to become monotonous by frequent repetition.[8]

Some good advice there!

There are two kinds of extremes to be avoided. On the one hand, we shouldn't be so "flexible" that there is no discipline, no routine, and, very quickly no program. On the other hand, we need not hold to our "program" as rigidly as an athlete training for the Olympics does.

But this "other hand" raises a very interesting issue: Or, *maybe* we *should* be as "rigid" as the serious athlete. Paul uses language in the New Testament taken from just such games, and the life of the soldier, and uses them as images of the Christian life. Think about this rather incredible statement:

> Do you not know that those who run in a race all run, but *only* one receives the prize? Run in such a way that you may win. And everyone who competes in the games exercises self-control in all things. They then *do it* to receive a perishable wreath, but we an imperishable. Therefore I run in such a way, as not without aim; I box in such a way, as not beating the air; but I buffet my body and make it my slave, lest possibly, after I have preached to others, I myself should be disqualified (1 Cor. 9:24-27).

We find it very difficult to even read this passage without being humbled, or to imagine others not having the same reaction.[9] If young people can exert such self-control, discipline, and denial with regard to the modern Olympic games (or everyday ordinary high school track or foot-

---

[8]Robert Richardson, *Memoirs of Alexander Campbell* (Nashville: Gospel Advocate Company, 1956), Vol. 2, p. 301.

[9]See also Colossians 2:18; Galatians 2:2; 2 Timothy 4:7; Hebrews 12:1, Ephesians 6:10-17.

ball), why shouldn't they be so encouraged for a "spiritual" goal today?

The "key" here with regard to flexibility is to avoid legalism or a strict authoritarianism in matters of time, format, and style in family worship. After all, this doesn't work for the church, why should we think it would work in the family. "Severe restrictions" may hinder rather than help to achieve productivity in family relations.

(2) *Practicality*: One of the reasons our "New Year's Resolutions" seem to almost always fail is that we think we can overhaul our entire lives by setting some (usually unrealistic) principles down and have them all in place all in one day. Very often such resolutions are neither realistic or practical. We shouldn't "bite off more than we can chew" (either in terms of time or content) at first. Family worship should be "fitted" to the needs and developmental levels of the family members involved. This is not to say that "high level" discussions of theological issues are not good or important for older children and parents.

(3) *Naturalness*: As Deuteronomy 6 clearly implies, family worship should not only involve formal teaching, but it should be normal and natural as well, involving every aspect of life. ". . . and you shall teach them diligently . . . and shall talk of them when you sit in your house and when you walk [drive] by the way and when you lie down and when you rise up" (vs. 7).[10] Family worship need not be formal or "a big deal" all the time. Too much fanfare — broadcasting, pushing, propaganda — can make it appear to be anything but a normal part of Christian family life.

Example: Taking a few extra seconds when you are

---

[10]Besides Deuteronomy 6, other Scriptures that might be used naturally in or to underline the importance of family worship are: Zech. 7; Matt. 18:20; Mark 9:36-37; Eph. 6:1-9; 2 Tim. 3:14-17. With any Scripture passage you might want to start with general overview and then go back to use one verse at a time for a session.

about to start a trip to check if anyone has forgotten anything (as most families do), to fasten seat belts, and to say a short prayer of thanks and for a safe trip can keep the family focused, as well as help the children see that we are putting the trip in God's hands in a real sense. We are trusting Him for our fun and safety! *Little moment by little moment "interjections" of "spiritual" emphasis can teach more than devotions that are boring and lifeless!*

If Possible, Start When the Children Are Young

Of course it is best if we make family worship a "lifestyle" and start as early in the lives of our children as possible. The earlier they hear God's Word "fall upon their minds and hearts," the better it will be. Start with Scriptures that teach central themes like John 3:16 and the Scripture about Jesus and little children (Mark 9:36-37). You might start with shortened versions that they can understand. Remember young children have short attention spans. But here we must not underestimate the importance of the Holy Spirit to "root it" in their minds "by His wisdom, even though the child . . . has as yet no thinking powers to hold it."[11]

For centuries, Christian leaders have thought that having their young children memorize select Scripture had an effect beyond measure. Thomas and Jane Campbell had a rule:

> . . . that every member [of the family] should memorize, during each day, some portion of the Bible, to be recited at evening worship. Long passages were often thus recited, but if only a single verse was correctly repeated by the smaller children, it was received with encouraging approbation. Attention was usually called to the important facts or truths

---

[11] Norman V. Williams, *The Christian Home* (Chicago: Moody Press, 1952), p. 118.

The Family and Worship

presented in each recitation, questions were asked in regard to them, and appropriate remarks briefly offered. Finally, the Scriptures repeated during the week were again rehearsed on the evening of the Lord's day.[12]

The Campbell household must have been an exciting place to be.

The wisdom of Psalm 119: 9-11,

> How can a young man keep his way pure? By keeping it according to Thy word. With all my heart I have sought Thee; Do not let me wander from Thy commandments. Thy word I have treasured in my heart, That I may not sin against Thee.

can be started much earlier than many realize. A Scripture memorization program (like the Navigators, for example) might be beneficial — just be careful not to "overload" the children.[13]

The earlier our children are immersed in our love and the love of God and the Scripture, the more you will be building positive discipline and the less you will need punishment! Williams is not far off the mark when he says:

> The greatest tragedy in Christendom and to the cause of Christ is the *utter waste of the first four golden years of opportunity*. The child in the tender . . . impressionable state he is in from one day to four years is the golden opportunity for every parent to lay the Word of God deep in his life as a firm foundation for all

---

[12]Richardson, *Memoirs of Alexander Campbell*, Vol. 1, pp. 35-36. For an introduction to the thought and legacy of Alexander Campbell see Miethe, *The Philosophy and Ethics of Alexander Campbell: From the Context of American Religious Thought, 1800-1866*, Ph.D. Dissertation, University of Southern California, 1984.

[13]Also remember that as important and valuable as Scripture memorization can be, it doesn't take the place of serious study into the *meaning* of those memorized Scriptures!

[14]Williams, *The Christian Home*, p. 121.

else that shall follow.[14]

Certainly, medical doctors and child psychologists are beginning again to emphasize the importance of the very early days and months in the formation of the brain pathways, thinking skills, attitudes, and even later behavior.

Very Common Mistakes

There are so many possible little "traps" when we think about either personal devotions or family worship. Avoid the mistake of using inadequate adult devotional material and difficult Bible translations that don't communicate with children. Don't cause the family to feel guilty when devotions are missed once in a while. Perhaps the biggest "death trap" for family devotions or worship is a careless lack of planning, frequent forgetting, or gross irrelevance of the subject matter! Hardly anything makes this important and happy part of family life into more of a real chore. This careless attitude clearly shows your children just how *un*important family worship really is — to you at least.

Some Old Suggestions

Before we actually give some suggestions with regard to family worship, we are reminded of a powerful statement:

> Children are far more perceptive in spiritual matters than adults sometimes realize. They do not respond merely to the words and formal beliefs of their parents. They sense the inner *spirit* of the faith, and that is what they react to. Oftentimes young people who rebel against the Christian Faith are not rebelling against God at all. They have never had an actual encounter with the Living God to rebel against. They are rebelling against a dead religious

---

[15]Christenson, *The Christian Family*, p. 159.

The Family and Worship

formalism which merely imposes upon them a certain set of rules or rituals.[15]

You would do well to "burn" this into your mind! If your children sense — and they will — that your actions are really out of little more than a dead formalism, and the "rituals" therefore have little or no meaning, this may be worse than doing nothing!

Again, we must not forget the freedom we have in this area to be innovative and to meet your family's particular schedule and needs. But here are some "tried and true" suggestions many have felt were helpful:

(1) Praying parents need to "develop" praying children! Unquestionably, the "secret" to praying children is parents who themselves pray while alone, and with their children. Sincere, honest, open prayer is an essential starting point. We have observed parents teaching their children to pray almost as early as they were capable of controlling their heads enough to bow and their hands enough to hold them together. More about prayer in chapter 9. But suffice it here to say we are *not* talking about "chanting" — or repeating — a standard mealtime grace.

(2) Have a regular plan of reading and explaining the Scriptures morning and evening if at all possible. How can we persuade children that God is important, if we never give Him any time? It is most important that we be loving and diligent — "when you sit in the house, when you're out for a walk, when you go to bed, when you get up." It may be helpful, especially if small children are involved, to start by reading a Bible story — perhaps, from a children's Bible story book — as the basis or beginning of worship or devotions. We must make the Scriptures an important and regular part of our children's lives (Psalm 119:9, 11).

(3) "Invocation" is a part of worship often forgotten by the family. You say, "But if God is always present with us,

Serving Christ: A Family Affair

why do we have to 'invoke' His presence." We don't. But it can be helpful for all involved to remind us to "acknowledge" His presence. In fact, it sets the stage, the tone for this most important realization: the presence of Our Heavenly Father. It is certainly respectfully appropriate to both acknowledge His presence and to invite Him to be a part of a special time. The more we believe in His presence, the more "secure" we will feel.

(4) Singing can be a positive reinforcement of commitments and attitudes. It is also a very powerful way to direct attitudes and to express emotions in a positive way. When Terry used to take our son off to preschool he would sing songs that helped put both John Hayden and Terry in a positive mood for the day ahead. Singing can be a mirror of the attitude and health of the soul. Singing can be a way to lift the "mundane" of everyday experience to the level of appreciation for, and thanks, to God for life itself.

(5) Families find dramatization to be fun and to contribute to family worship. (Many congregations are discovering this in corporate worship as well.) Bible stories can be used this way. Read the story and let the whole family act it out. Look for the element of conflict in the story and build the drama around that point. God told the children of Israel to re-enact the great events of deliverance from Egypt (Exod. 13:5-10). One of the simplest, and most meaningful rituals — the symbol of family unity before the Lord — properly interpreted, is joining hands around the table for prayer.

(6) One suggestion is that children take one verse of Psalm 119, with its 176 verses, every morning to mediate upon and to go over that Psalm twice in a year because this "will bring you to be in love with all the rest of

---

[16]So it is reported that Philip Henry (who was educated at Christ Church, Oxford), Matthew Henry's father, taught his children.

The Family and Worship

Scripture."[16] It is true that Psalm 119 is powerful and full of wonderful truth. It has been called meditations and prayers relating to the Law of God. But it also reminds us of God's faithfulness and "lovingkindness."

(7) Some practice what is often called an "unbroken circle" around the breakfast or dinner table, where each family member repeats a verse of Scripture,[17] after which hands are joined and the Lord's Prayer is repeated,[18] and then one member ends with a few words of prayer. It is hard to overestimate the importance of knowing Scripture. We have many powerful stories of soldiers in wartime, and who have spent months and years in captivity, who credit their sanity and survival to the Scriptures they had memorized as small children which again came to mind in great times of need!

(8) When taking trips, break up the monotony, again, with "spiritual" moments. Have light family discussions about family things, instead of the children playing games all the time. Many potentially important family moments can be wasted because we simply don't think of doing "spiritual" things. Since you have to drive, and concentrate on the traffic, you may be more likely to actually let the children talk — and maybe even listen to them as well. Stop the car every so often not only to get out and stretch, but to say a little prayer or sing a song. Make God an important part of your life as naturally as you can by thinking of Him often. Redeem the time!

---

[17]In some families, children under four or five are allowed to say the same verse for a month (actually a good idea). Children under eight must have a new verse every week; over twelve must have a new verse every morning and it must not be repeated within thirty days. But make up guidelines that work for you.

[18]We understand there are many theologians and ministers — Terry is one — who say that the Lord's Prayer was intended to be a model for prayer and not a prayer to be repeated at rote as it were. That being acknowledged, one could hardly do better than to pray with intent and feeling the words of Jesus' prayer.

Serving Christ: A Family Affair

(9) Write your children little, short love notes from you — and or God (these can be the words of Jesus, etc.) — and remind them just how special they are, how important their relationship to the Lord is, how much **fun** it is to be a Christian, etc. At the end of the day, and maybe even of life itself, it may well be that the important moments weren't the "big" ones, but the little ones. Taking the time to do the "little things" to acknowledge God, your faith, your love, will help form an "attitude of mind" in life and provide the mortar that will make sense out of life itself.

(10) Take short walks with the family, or individual family members, and talk about "spiritual" things. During these short walks you will not only have the wonderful privilege of experiencing the beauty of God's creation, but also have time to share in spite of a hectic schedule. Some of our most enduring family memories have been of such walks just around the neighborhood, or in Creve Coeur Park, or walking in the woods of the Blue Ridge mountains, or on the beach, and *sharing each other* and with each other. What more wonderful time to talk of God and His importance to you and your lives.

(11) Most families have special traditions at times like Thanksgiving or Christmas. There is nothing wrong with these, no matter what certain "fundamentalists" may tell you. Because Terry didn't want Christmas to be "secular" and "materialistic," we didn't have a Christmas tree for the first few years of our marriage. Then, we realized that the issue wasn't how the world celebrated holidays, but how we did; nor what the symbols meant to society, but what they meant to us. So we have tried to form family traditions that take advantage of national holidays and also really witness to the Christian truths surrounding them. But why only have "celebrations" in connection with holidays? Why not develop special times for *your* family and their Christian commitment. These could be

The Family and Worship

practiced weekly, monthly, seasonally, or in conjunction with or around birthdays, anniversaries, etc.

In general, the more you can laugh and have fun as a part of family devotions or "spiritual" things, the more the children will enjoy them and the more they will see them as an important, exciting part of normal family life. Remember: You can hardly expect your children to want to spend time with you, or learn from you; when you make it obvious that you don't want to spend time with them, or aren't really interested in their fears, anxieties, everyday problems, hopes, or dreams.

It can be important to "start the day off right." Above all, family devotions, family worship, or the "family altar," should tie a family together in love and holiness! Again, the "key" is to make whatever you do a natural part of your "lifestyle," not something that is (obviously to the children) contrived and tacked on as an afterthought. Consequently, we must be very careful that whatever we do is interesting, informative, and even exciting, so that it doesn't have the exact opposite effect to the one we intend.

CHAPTER SIX
Church Leaders and Their Families

Unfortunately, one still hears ministers' children referred to in a "negative" way as "preachers' kids" or "PKs" (and missionaries' kids" as MKs) because of the stereotype that these children are frequently rather "unruly." Naturally, the question comes to mind, "Why does this seem to be so often true?" Maybe you have heard the quip (brief, witty remark delivered offhand), "The reason the minister's kids have behavior problems is because they have to play with the elder's and deacon's kids." All "kidding" aside, there is absolutely no question that church leaders — ministers, elders, deacons, church school teachers, even "average" Christians — have a responsibility to live in such a way as to be able to serve as examples for the church and to the community.

As a minister, Terry feels that the "truth" which forms the basis for this unfortunate stereotype is the fact that the demands of the ministry — which are great indeed — are so often used as an "excuse" by the minister to cheat his own children of time and attention. Tragically, this is how it sometimes breaks down when the minister is confronted with the need to do some "soul searching" with regard to what went wrong in the family. In fact, the "higher" the leadership responsibility, the more important the example of the family relationship! One of the wisest pieces of advice Terry was ever given as a minister was this: "You take care of the depth of your ministry and let God take care of its breadth." We are called to be faithful to Christ, not "successful" in the eyes of the world!

Serving Christ: A Family Affair

Church Leaders in the New Testament

When we look at the structure of the church in the New Testament, we see that the elders and deacons are to be examples in, or more importantly *models of* Christian living to the church and the world. This is one of the qualifications which make one fit for serving as a leader. In God's Word there are clearly specified "credentials" with regard to the family for church leaders. These indicate that the total family is to be involved in service to Christ and the church. It *should* go without saying that church leaders should serve as an example not only for church members, but to people outside the church.

First Timothy 3:4-5 teaches that one of the qualifications for elder, or overseer, is a family life that is exemplary, i.e., serving as a sample, typical, a model. "He must be one who manages his own household well, keeping his children under control with all dignity (but if a man does not know how to manage his own household, how will he take care of the church of God?)" The noun "dignity" points to both parents' attitudes. "Dignity" is the quality of being gentle (noble), honorable, self-respecting. The idea is that strict discipline must be maintained, but without fuss or resort to violence. Surely, this "dignity" and "discipline" applies to the wife and mother as well. We also read in 1 Timothy, "Women must likewise be dignified, not malicious gossips, but temperate, faithful in all things" (vs. 11).

The list of qualifications for elders in Titus closely resembles that prescribed in 1 Timothy 3:2-7. Titus 1:6 specifically states that an overseer is to be one "whose children believe and are not open to the charge of being wild and disobedient" (NIV). The elder's children thus provide an important and useful test of their father's qualifications for service. Could this be any clearer? They should be believers, sharing their father's faith in Christ, and in their daily conduct the children should not be chargeable with "loose living" or being "out of control."[1] A man who cannot bring up his own children as Christians certainly cannot "bring up a congregation." Clearly we see that the leaders of our churches, who are examples for the families of the church, are to make serving Christ a family affair. No other conclusion is possible.

This prerequisite for leadership in the church is such "common sense" one wonders why it had to be spelled out at all? And yet church after church ignores both the common sense and biblical mandate. A seminary professor of Terry's used to say that the real problem with the biblical qualifications for elders and deacons, indeed, for Christian leaders in general, was not that they were too high, but why the standards were so low. With the exception of "not being a novice in the faith" the same standards are expected of each and every believer, he would say. A claim of the churches of Christ (the non-instrumental branch of the Restoration Movement) is that they take the office and role of elder much more seriously than other groups. Terry has ministered with and to elders in numerous churches of Christ and finds this gross generalization just not true. The "quality" of the eldership in this group is *no better* on the whole when compared to the beliefs, etc., of the average member of the congregation.[2]

---

[1] Greek *asotia*: the cognate adverb is used in Luke 15:13 of the prodigal son's "riotous living."

[2] Terry's experience is that elders — even with earned doctorates in other than biblical fields — in the churches of Christ are not necessarily any more "literate" theologically than their counterparts in other wings of the Restoration Movement. Often, an elder's appointment was rather political. In fact, a relatively "weak" eldership in the biblical sense is one reason why the churches of Christ, and other groups as well, are not progressing. The truth of the matter is that churches of Christ have almost all crossed over to a professional clergy / laity system, perhaps without even realizing it.

Many churches of Christ congregational leaders view "taking the eldership more seriously" as interpreting the scriptural qualifications

Serving Christ: A Family Affair

Virtually the same domestic qualifications are recorded for deacons. "Let deacons be husbands of only one wife, and good managers of their children and their own households" (1 Tim. 3:12). Thus, deacons also should give proof of their fitness for ministry, i.e., service, by having families that are "managed" according to God's plan. And, yet, if some tend to take this requirement lightly for elders, often it is totally ignored for deacons. Surely this connotes a family involved in service to or ministry for Christ as a total unit.

Leaders Must "Embody" the Word

The life and problems of many local congregations are reflected in microcosm in those of the individual family — and, of course, it is also true that the congregation is a macrocosm of problems found in individual families. Without question, Scripture teaches that the same qualities are needed for leadership in both. Even if it isn't intuitively — incredibly — obvious that if the parents can't lead their own family, they are not going to be able to lead the church; the New Testament makes it clear that they are disqualified for leadership if they cannot effectively lead their own family!

---

in some very incorrect ways. For example, the phrase "believing children" is used to argue (not only that all men who have no children are disqualified from the eldership, or those whose children have not yet been immersed, but also) that those men who have only *one* child — no matter how "spectacular" a Christian that child is — are scripturally disqualified from ever being elders! It must be added, that some of their better educated scholars, serving at some of their more conservative schools, know this is not proper reasoning.

In my experience [Terry's] many of the churches of Christ have serious problems with understanding hermeneutical principles. In this, part of the reason is one of their "great strengths"; i.e., in developing a good liberal arts college system, they have neglected teaching logic, philosophy, and advanced biblical interpretation skills. At many of their schools, even some of the most advanced and progressive, not even one course in philosophy, much less logic, is required.

Church Leaders and Their Families

This seriousness in choosing leaders who can be examples is also clearly present in the missionary strategy of the New Testament church. Stress was put not just on hearing the Word, but the on embodiment of the Word in the life of the missionary. In 1 Thessalonians 2:13, we read that when they "received . . . the word of God's message, [they] accepted it not as the word of men, but for what it really is, the word of God, which also performs its work in [those] who believe." If the "Word of God" is believed it will perform its work on the heart and mind of the one who believes. "Transformation" — in terms of faithfulness, not "success" — is then a clear indication of the embodiment.

This embodiment of the Word must be especially true in the lives of church leaders. Paul had both taught and modeled ministry to young Timothy, and as a result Timothy was ready to progress to his own ministry. We need far more "ministerial internships" today than we have, so that young ministers can be with ministers who do embody the Word. Timothy and Titus were instructed to choose men who exemplified Christian maturity. Their attitude and behavior were to be consistent with the faith if they were to serve as leaders for the young church. We also need "leadership internships" in our churches today.

"Those who were simply able to mouth Christian teaching were not acceptable as leaders; in leaders the spoken Word and the lived Word must correspond." Richards goes on to ask:

> Why this biblical emphasis on correspondence of Word and life? *Because the communication of Christian faith has always been a matter of communicating lifestyle. The total way of life — those values and attitudes and behavior that bundled together with beliefs constitute the growing person — must give living expression in the world to the reality revealed in God's Word.*[3]

---

[3]Larry Richards, "How the Church Can Help the Family Fact the Future" in Collins' *Facing the Future: The Church and Family Together*, p. 14.

Serving Christ: A Family Affair

A powerful truth. We are not talking about some sort of unrealistic "perfection," but a constant attempt to grow and mature in our understanding and in living out what we understand.

Paul tells the Philippians and us, "For I am confident of this very thing, that He who began a good work in you will perfect it until the day of Christ Jesus" (1:6). This is a promise we must claim for ourselves and for our leaders. Claiming this promise most probably will not happen by accident or apathy. Call it the path of least resistance, laziness, accident, or apathy. The truth of the matter is we choose the areas of the intellect in which we will be ignorant just as surely as we choose those in which we will be knowledgeable, only maybe more so. The two greatest sins of Christians (almost unforgivable sins) must be apathy and willful ignorance. We mentioned, in the "Introduction," the disease of mediocrity which must never be allowed to emasculate the church. So allow Christ to work in your life and in your family!

The Family of God

So, church leaders must exemplify and embody Christianity in their families or they shouldn't be leaders in the family of God, the church. This "exemplification" must be real, not just programmatic. For example:

> . . . a local church may sponsor a marriage enrichment seminar. But if the pastor is too busy for his own family and if the church program constantly breaks up family unity by involving different family members most nights of the week, the people will come to place a low, not a high, priority on the family. The life-style of the church and its families communicates more effectively than words.[4]

---

[4]Ibid.

Church Leaders and Their Families

We have experienced so many similar situations. By far most of us witness to what we really are far more by example than by spoken word! Sometimes the "darker" side of the reality is a rather subtle realization that what we say really conflicts with what we program.

The question arises, "Exactly how does anyone, church officer or not, model what they believe?" Strange as it may seem to "postmodern" ears, God gave us, as we have already seen, the answer to this question through Moses in Deuteronomy 6:4-9.[5] We like J.B. Phillips, *The New Testament in Modern English*, in which he paraphrases Peter's instructions to leaders entrusted with the flock:

> Now may I who am myself an elder say a word to you my fellow elders? I speak as one who actually saw Christ suffer, and as one who will share with you the glories that are to be unfolded to us. I urge you then to see that your "flock of God" is properly fed and cared for. Accept the responsibility of looking after them willingly and not because you can't get out of it, doing your work not for what you can make, but because you are really concerned for their well-being. *You should aim not at being 'little tin gods' but as examples of Christian living in the eyes of the flock committed to your charge.* And then, when the chief shepherd reveals himself, you will receive that crown of glory which cannot fade" (1 Pet. 5:1-4, emphasis added).[6]

Evidently, Peter had a problem with the seriousness of elders even in the New Testament. Most tragically, we have known more than our share of "little tin" men in the church who thought they were really BIG! In a church which claims to be one of the biggest in the coun-

---

[5] See the section in chapter 2 on Deuteronomy 6:4-9.

[6] J. B. Phillips, *The New Testament in Modern English* (New York: The Macmillan Company, 1966).

try, what the leaders model — so inconsistent with what they say — has had tragic consequences in the life of that body.

Again, as the Scripture indicates, the first aspect they *must* model is a real Christian family life. Many of our church leaders need to very carefully reassess their priorities. The "quality" or "attribute" which made them eligible to be, and should have been seriously considered before they became, church leaders in the first place was that they managed their own households well. And, yet, too often the "ministry" is given priority over a man's family. Sort of a strange contradiction, isn't it? In fact, just the opposite should be the case: the more a person wants to be a leader of the church, the more that person must look to, and take care of, his or her family. This must involve more than just spending time at home. *The family must be shared with the church so that the church family can see the individual leader's family lifestyle and have a living model after which to pattern their families.*

We know of one minister who thinks that Christian "hospitality" begins at home and is an important part of his ministry. He and his wife and children invite a couple or two from the church into their home each week to spend an evening of talking and sharing. Nothing "elaborate" is planned for the guests. It is simply an attempt to allow the members of his "church family" to get to know him and his family better, in a more personal way. Rather an interesting take on "pastoral visitation," don't you think? Instead of always going to his members' homes (though this can also be important), he invites his members to make a visit with his family. This has actually done wonders for that church.

In all churches, surely, there are "committees" assigned to focus on important aspects of the life of the church. As both a minister and an academician, one of Terry's favorite sayings is, "In Heaven, there will be no commit-

Church Leaders and Their Families

tees." Terry prefers the "task force" model.[7] How about a family life task force? Shouldn't the place and needs of the family be constantly before the leadership? Over the years, depending on the "fad in fashion" different kinds of ministers have been called to serve as "second chair," e.g., associate minister, minister of education, youth minister, of counseling, of visitation, of evangelism, of the elderly, etc.

Nowadays, even *moderate size* churches have more than one professional staff member. But perhaps we could actually avoid the need for some of these if we have a "Minister of Family Life." Certain of these other duties naturally could fit with a particular minister's emphasis; for example, minister of family life and counseling make a "natural" combination. At the very least, having a family life minister could be a very important way to reinforce the importance of the family in the church.

One thing is absolutely clear. However well intentioned, or misguided, we must stop electing leaders who are not qualified, or who are not really serious about serving. Terry has "defined" an overseer thus: "An Elder: One who is willing to stand before the judgment bar of God and accept the responsibility for the spiritual life of a congregation."[8]

---

[7]In this model, a group is called together to perform a specific function and is called into existence only for that function. After the task is completed the committee is thanked for its service and "disbanded." When another need arises a new task force is called into being. This philosophy eliminates the need for large numbers of standing committees. Some of the task forces might need to "exist" long-term, but the membership should be rotated often enough to give individual members a break.

[8]Miethe, *Reflections*, Vol. 1.

CHAPTER SEVEN
Parenting: Some Practical Suggestions

We think it will be helpful here to give some rather succinct, practical suggestions for parenting. But before the practical advice, we are reminded of an interesting statement by Martin Luther about us "older folk":

> For what other purpose do we older folk exist than to care for, instruct and bring up the young? . . . But it is a sin and a disgrace that we must needs urge and be urged to train our children and youths and seek their best interests, when nature itself should drive us to do this and the examples even of the heathen afford us manifold instruction. . . . And *what would it profit us if we possessed and performed all else and became utter saints, and yet neglected the chief purpose of our life, namely, the care of the young? I believe also that among outward sins none so heavily burdens the world in the sight of God nor deserves such severe punishment as the sin we commit against our children by not giving them an education.* . . . [emphasis added].[1]

Powerfully put! But if we neglected our young, could we ever become "utter saints"? We think not! Tragically, even people in the church seem to have a different attitude today about parental responsibility than Luther!

1. Discipline is not the same as punishment! Hopefully this will *imprint on the mind.* Yet so many of us have grown up thinking of the two as the same, with "disci-

---

[1]Martin Luther, "To the Councilmen of All Cities in Germany That They Establish and Maintain Christian Schools," *Works of Martin Luther*, Vol. IV, pp. 106-124.

pline" equaling punishment. Therefore, it is so hard to "shake" this false comparison. Still, it is this very false comparison that causes much of our anguish with our children's behavior problems in the first place! Often, we wait until some action has occurred over and over again (or until such behavior becomes too unbearable) and then *punish* our children. We should have used discipline positively in the first place to have stopped the negative behavior as, or even before, it started. When discipline is properly exercised the need for punishment lessens.

A student of Terry's, a much older "nontraditional" student, asked him when he was making this point in one of his college classes, "But how can you discipline without punishment?" This question just illustrates the fact that many do not separate the two words. They see "discipline" as "punishment" and "punishment" as "discipline." Terry's answer was that the very best method of "discipline" is love. Loving your children and assuring they know that you love them unconditionally, yet that certain attitudes and actions are simply unacceptable in the family is the very best basis for discipline! Not only is "love" a far better method of discipline, but it reaps much greater results and, as we have said, actually drastically reduces the need for punishment. (More on this in chapter 8, in the section "Discipline and Punishment are NOT the Same.")

2. Be consistent. It is hard to say too much about the importance of consistency. "Consistency" can be and is a very important element in successful discipline. For you see, effective discipline also enables you to then avoid the need for punishment. Consistency helps our children know clearly what is expected and encourages them to behave appropriately in a given situation. It means our children can *develop a sense of trust in us* as parents and can rely on us — with experience — that we will not only be consistent, but fair as well.

Parenting: Some Practical Suggestions

Of course, consistency demands communication within the entire family structure. This is so very important! It is impossible to be "consistent" if we do not communicate clearly and effectively so that all family members know the "rules of the household," the expectations in a given situation, and the lines of authority (See #4 below). Very simply, don't say one thing then ten minutes later say or allow the opposite. When we do this our children have us right where they want us. When you say "no" mean no!

We have seen what seems like legions of parents who let their children control a given situation by almost constant "nagging" all the while the parents are saying "no." The children know that they don't really mean no because the parents haven't "blown up" yet; no confrontation has happened. We might add, it is almost inevitably such parents who cannot seem to understand why they have trouble "controlling" their children! You see, the child or children know whether "no" *means* no or not by clearly observing a long history of family action. "No" means no only when you get mad and yell, "NO!" But if this is how it works in your home you have lost the battle before it began. You are *not* "disciplining" your child or children and you have set the stage rather certainly for the need for punishment!

Also, the number of children complicates a given situation and increases the need for consistency and good communication. We have kept all the children from a large family for days at a time, so we *know* the amount of effort to do anything with a large number of children doesn't increase in a simple "one plus one" numerical fashion. Every time you add a child it seems like you have an exponential increase; that is, the factor of difficulty in doing a particular task is multiplied! We can hear all you parents out there with large families saying, "Amen!"

But why is the number of children all of a sudden

Serving Christ: A Family Affair

important here to consistency and effective communication? If parents can do these things well with large families, there is no excuse for us with small ones! We knew one dear family with six children very close in age who never, except maybe once or twice in the beginning, had a problem with what "no" means. They were a close, loving Christian family — what all Christian families should *work* to become. And it does take work. Here was no "overbearing" parent, either husband or wife. Yet when they said "no, that is not acceptable behavior" those six children knew to stop immediately. We never heard them have to repeat themselves. The parents were lovingly consistent. They communicated clearly and constantly with their children. The children *knew* what was expected of them in a given situation. If they forgot for a moment as children will sometimes do, all the parent had to say was, "No, that is not acceptable behavior" (in this situation in their family). You can imagine what a pleasure it was to be around that family! They were an incredible witness to all who had the opportunity to know them.

3. Set reasonable fences. Make reasonable demands. Don't act in anger. How often do we as parents perch ourselves out there on the end of the proverbial limb and then proceed to saw it off with us on the wrong side of the cut! How many times have you reacted in anger because your child, while playing with Jimmy, did something you told him or her not to do. When you found out you shouted, "You're never going to play with Jimmy again!" Now, Jimmy just happens to be your child's best friend and the child of your best friend, or close neighbor. There you go with the saw again! You have just successfully broken one — really several — of the beginning rules of parenting!

Make reasonable demands. One of the problems parents run into, often "head-on," is that they aren't "in

Parenting: Some Practical Suggestions

tune" with their children enough to know what can reasonably be expected of them. We must be in tune with them developmentally, with regard to their personal emotional makeup, etc. When we expect too much out of our children, we are only setting ourselves up for disappointment and them up for failure! Ironically, it is often when we have offspring who are usually extremely good, tender, sensitive children who occasionally do "bad" things, that we as parents overreact to something which is in reality quite small. In these times we tend to overreact because we are so used to just how wonderful our children usually are that we take it for granted. It doesn't help anyone if we overreact to behavioral problems — small ones or big ones! "Swatting flies" with an iron skillet only makes a bigger mess for you to eventually have to clean up!

If we don't set reasonable fences and make reasonable demands, we have already undermined that fragile and wonderful *trust* that makes parenting not only possible, but a joy. (See #10 below.) The best way to insure that, as a parent, you set reasonable fences and make reasonable demands is to have thought out beforehand how you are going to react in certain circumstances. For example, it would be immensely helpful if you and your spouse would sit down and think through possible situations and categorize them from most serious down to most minor and have a corresponding list of possible punishments that go with each category of misbehavior.[2] Yes, it helps — to put it mildly — if parents *think* about being parents!

---

[2]See Hugh Jolly, *The First Five Years: Answers Questions from Parents* (Minneapolis: Winston Press, 1984) is an authentic, practical, beautifully illustrated guide on rearing children from birth to five. Some call it a "must." Nina R. Lief and M. E. Fahs, *The Second Year of Life: A Guide for Parenting* (New York: Dodd, Mead and Co., 1984) is important for all parents as well as ministers and counselors.

Serving Christ: A Family Affair

Don't act, or react, in anger! Wait till you cool off if you can't deal with the situation without anger. But don't wait too long. When our children see us react to a discipline problem with anger, it not only makes us appear rather "childlike" ourselves, but undermines the trust that is, again, so important in building discipline. When they see us react angrily often, it doesn't take long for them to grow to fear us. Especially in dealing with discipline problems, they should be motivated to love us. Fear can be a factor for behavioral change, up to a point; but we by no means believe it is the only way to encourage change and it certainly is not the best. *Ruling a child, especially a very sensitive one, with a "heavy hand" can do great damage to the psyche*!

4. Never undermine the other parent's authority. Have the "lines of authority" clear beforehand. Above all support each other. So many times we have seen situations where one parent says one thing and the other another. Often, children learn very early to play parents off against each other! Dad is asked, but his answer is not what is wanted. So, off they go to Mom. Mom, not knowing that Dad has already been asked, gives a different answer. Then, they go back to Dad and say, "Mom said it was O.K." The children have you right where they want you!

Whatever the scenario, some rather simple precautions can solve this problem long before it becomes a problem. (a) Have a *strict understanding, an unbreakable commitment* between parents that one will never undermine the others' authority! (b) Let the children know that going from parent to parent will not be tolerated; it is not acceptable behavior. Something as simple as saying, "Have you talked to Dad about this yet?" will solve the problem. If they lie to you, then you may have a more serious problem, but you will not have to worry about contradicting your mate. (c) If as parents, you disagree seriously *do not show it to your children*! Simply say to them, "Mom and I

Parenting: Some Practical Suggestions

need to talk a little about this before we give you an answer. We will get back to you very soon." Of course, you must get back to them soon! Often we parents, are our own worst enemies because our children "use their heads" more in a given situation than we do! Certainly, if this is the case you, as parents, are not going to engender trust and confidence in your guidance, judgment, and maturity.

5. Deal with children on their level. It is not enough to just give commands, even "consistent" ones. If you are going to "build" (the key word here) a workable system of discipline *they must understand to their ability* not only that you love them unconditionally, but that the "fences" you set are what you truly believe is best for them at the time. The more love they feel from you, the more confidence and trust you have engendered in them *for your judgment* the less problem you will have with behavior.

If a small child is "unruly" while waiting in a long restaurant line, under no circumstances is it appropriate behavior to jerk them up and whip them in front of everyone! On more than one occasion, we have seen "Christian" families do this to our absolute horror and the horror of almost everyone else — Christian or not — in line! Once we witnessed a man who holds a Th.D. (Doctor of Theology) degree and who teaches theology at a Christian university do this to his two- to three-year-old! Surely, it doesn't take a "rocket scientist" — in the current vernacular — to see that this is most inappropriate behavior. Yet the "theologian" thought it was the "Christian" thing to do! Surely, *if* punishment was absolutely necessary it would have made much more sense to have taken the child outside, or somewhere with some privacy, to administer the punishment.[3]

---

[3]We might add that in this particular case we were with the other couple in line (again, much to our embarrassment), standing right next to them, and *we* had not noticed any behavior on the part of the young child to merit punishment at all.

Serving Christ: A Family Affair

Oh sure, you can frighten a child into submission, at least for a time. But all along the road you will destroy the self-image, individual strength, and ultimately, the child's ability to make wise independent judgments. We have seen parents who "ruled the roost" with a subtle — or not so subtle — "brutality" and can't think of a single case where such parents did not reap what they had sown in later years! Eventually children under such a regimen will rebel or have very damaged psyches — likely both!

A three-year-old will need to understand on his or her level. Understanding "age appropriateness" is very important for a parent. As children grow into adolescents, a great deal of discussion with them will be not only appropriate, but necessary. The more you have practiced loving consistent discipline which builds your children's confidence and trust in your judgment, the less "arguing" you will get from them as they grow older. After all, don't children have a "right" to expect their parents to be wiser and more mature than they?[4] Which brings us to suggestion number six.

6. Yet deal with them as an adult. Don't react like a child yourself. Sometimes all we show our children is a much bigger child when we react to them! Reacting to their action with great anger will probably only have negative consequences in the long run *both for them and for you*! As children grow older, and more mature, some actual negotiation may be appropriate with regard to "fences." Help your children to understand, always!

---

[4]Yet, tragically, the fact that the parents often aren't "wise and more mature" is the root of the problem in the first place. Grievously, today we have thousands of *children* — babies really — having babies. Often, these "unwanted" pregnancies, with children as young as 11 or 12, are really intentional. You see, these children want someone to love them unconditionally and someone they can love, too! Tragically, in almost every case, 12 or so years later the cycle just repeats itself because children were not meant to raise children, nor are they capable.

Parenting: Some Practical Suggestions

Bear in mind, parents are not always correct, not infallible either! If you make a mistake, admit it. Tell them you aren't perfect. Ultimately, this will *build* their confidence in you! One of the most comforting — yes comforting — things we have ever said to our child was, "I am sorry. I was wrong. Please forgive me!" Terry [being the one who needed to most — TLM add], often apologized to our son even when John Hayden was quite young. Terry felt quite strongly that it was important for our son to know how much he was loved; but also that we not only made mistakes, but were willing to admit our error, correct it, and were genuinely sorry for it!

7. Follow-up is important. Explain, communicate, love, share. It is hard to make too much of the "C" word, or the "L" word! Parents not only have an obligation before God, but a glorious privilege to teach, inform, show their affection, and to give of every aspect of their being to the children. In reality, it is like saying that the church should witness. The problem with the church is not that it does not witness. Fortunately or unfortunately, the church is always witnessing — to what it is and to what it is not, to what it should be and isn't, or to what it should be and is! People outside the church see this witness, positive or negative, clearly. Parents *do* give of who and what they really are to their children! Unfortunately, again, often the parents who are in need of counseling/help themselves speak, by example, most strongly of who they are to their children.

Often we do much more to reinforce negative behavior than positive. A television commercial shows a father entering his teenage son's room having found his son's drug paraphernalia. "Who taught you to do that?" demands the father angrily. "You, you did," said the son. Then a voice says, "Parents who do drugs have children who do drugs." Certainly, not all parents who do drugs have children who do, and just because the children do drugs doesn't mean their parents did. Yet the general truth of the commercial rings with an almost deafening roar. Even when we are thinking least about the possibility (maybe even more so, then), our children are observing us and learning from us! Many of us complain bitterly because we don't have any influence over our children when very possibly these very complainers have affected their children the most — often negatively — because they haven't paid the price to be an important part of their children's lives, to gently mold them in a positive way![5]

If we really want our children to grow up as strong and sensitive, responsible and giving, independent and caring, dedicated Christian adults; it will help *immensely* if we are such adults ourselves. When they see *us as positive models of everything we expect them to be* as they are growing up, we will be molding them in positive ways! We must be loving enough and responsible enough ourselves to be patiently, intimately involved in our children's lives throughout their growing years, not just "passive observers" who happen to live in the same house. This is not easy! It takes almost as much work as it does to keep your love alive, for your marriage to work in the first place.

Sometimes this patient loving must be done on *their* terms. We must really care for them, enough to allow them to be as important a part of our lives as we are in theirs. By the very nature of our "bigness" we are more

---

[5]Evelyn R. Duvall, *Parent and Teenager: Living and Loving* (Nashville: Broadman Press, 1976) abounds in practical suggestions explaining how parents may maximize the benefits and minimize the tensions of the teen years. Kathleen McCoy, *Coping with Teenage Depression: A Parent's Guide* (New York: New American Library, 1982). Vance Packard, *Our Endangered Children: Growing Up in a Changing World* (Boston: Little, Brown and Co., 1983) is for those involved with children in home, church, or school. Packard's material is always well researched and right on target. Merton Strommen, *Five Cries of Youth* (New York: Harper & Row, 1974).

Parenting: Some Practical Suggestions

important to them than they are to us, you see. How many times do you think it takes for a child who has asked and asked, "Daddy, are you listening?" to know you aren't, and to get the message that you don't really care? It doesn't take them long at all to see that that newspaper or TV or job is more important than they are! Follow-up is being willing to interact with them when they want and need you, not just when you want or need them! And, then, maybe — miracle of miracles, joy of joys — they will invite us to be a real part of their adult lives and families!

8. Try to constantly reinforce good behavior with positive praise. As we have seen, successful parenting is a "building" process. You do not become "failures" overnight, nor do you become successes in an instant. One very important aspect to raising children is not only that they feel constant security from their relationship with you, but that you give them that all-important positive praise they so need to feel confident in you and in themselves.

You know how you feel — that is before you become numb to it — when your boss at work doesn't at least occasionally "pat you on the back," at least acknowledge, if not "praise" your efforts. You feel unappreciated, used, and in your worst moments, maybe even guilty, or a personal failure. Just think how much more fragile children need to hear you tell them that they *are* good, that they *have done* good! When you give this much needed praise, they hear it as "I love you so-o-o-o much! *You* are really worthwhile!" This brings us to number nine.

9. Build a good self-image in your child! Most children grow up more in spite of their parents than because of their direct and positive influence. Children have such fragile egos. It would be hard to overemphasize the importance of building a good self-image in your young! How do you do this? In theology and philosophy, we learn that sometimes we can get at least a glimpse of what

Serving Christ: A Family Affair

something *is* if we first look to see what *it is not!*[6] Certainly, you do not build a good self-image by ignoring, putting down, or terrorizing your children.

Much of what we have already said in these suggestions for parenting are very important parts of building a good self-image; e.g., building a sense of confidence, trust, communication, love; in short that you love them and that *God loves them* — that they are special! What else is needed? At the very least, it is most important that you be aware of the need to do this in the first place! It is not likely that it will be done "by accident," and it is far too important to take the chance it will happen that way! Just being very consciously aware of the need may be half the battle. In other words, building a self-image is so important that you should "burn" it on to your foreheads, on the frontals of your mind! (See the material in this book on Deuteronomy 6:4-9 and further material on "(2) Building a good self-image" in chapter 8.)

10. Build a sense of confidence in you, that you are and always will be there for them. We have "hinted" at the importance of this time and again in the practical suggestions for parenting. Try not to keep putting them off. When you do, your child knows clearly just how important they are, and who or what is not a real priority to you! Communication is very important! All of the aspects mentioned in this chapter are *basic* to good parenting. None of this is going to be easy — if even possible — if you do not build a strong sense of confidence in your child that *you will be there for them no matter what!* To a large extent this confidence building is natural, starts at the birth of your child, and can be rebuilt effectively when breached occasionally. Remember, how

---

[6]In some theological systems, this is referred to as the "via negativa" or "by way of the negative." See Miethe, *The Compact Dictionary of Doctrinal Words*, p. 216.

Parenting: Some Practical Suggestions

important it is to be able to say we were wrong, we are sorry! (See suggestion #6.)

Some things have changed for the better! It used to be that a father had little to do with the actual birth process, but now he can be involved in almost every aspect. Of course, he still can't actually "feel" what it is like to give birth. Recently, our first grandchild was born. Our son was a very real help and comfort to our daughter as she went through a grueling 22 hours of labor. When Nicole finally went into the delivery room, John Hayden went right along in his green hospital clothes and white cap. A short time after the baby was born, John came into the nursery and proudly presented the new "bundle of joy" to the twenty-plus people waiting at three o'clock in the morning to see his debut!

It was immediately obvious that John and his new son, Britain Avery, had bonded. Britain was already responding to his father's kind, loving voice! Some will tell you this was possible so quickly because Britain recognized his father's voice already from when he was in the womb and father (and mother) talked to him, read to him, and had gently rubbed him for months already. Building a sense of confidence is natural and does begin very early. The "trick" is to keep it going and growing in as uninterrupted a fashion as is possible.

Terry has told the story many times of the minister who was playing with his young son. The son was sitting on the fender of a car. The father stretched out his arms and called to the child to jump. Just as the father said "jump," the mother, who was some distance away, called to the father and distracted him so that he looked away at precisely the moment the child jumped. The child fell to the ground. Though the child was not seriously hurt, the minister readily admitted that it was quite a while before his son would jump again when he held out his arms.

The confidence that made the child willing to jump

was based on the child's intimate knowledge of his parents. The child *knows* that he can trust father to catch him because the child has experienced his father's care and love. The trust is shaken after the child falls to the ground. It takes some time before that knowledge of trust can be restored. When our child trusts us it is because we have patiently, lovingly built a strong sense of confidence and trust in him or her! Yes, this kind of relationship is "natural" and begins very early, but it is also *absolutely essential to effective parenting*!

11. Above all, show love and acceptance even when punishment becomes necessary. *Always* make the distinction clear between disapproval of an action and approval of the child. Especially when punishment is necessary, the child should know all the more that he or she is loved. We can almost guarantee you that if your child knows how much you love them *even when you are in the middle of punishing them* you will not have to punish them very often! One of the very worst things you can do is to somehow cause your child to see your "love" and their "punishment" as opposite ends of a pole.

12. Especially in this day and age of hectic lifestyles, set aside some "quality time" for each family member, as well as for the family as a whole. This is not as hard as it may sound, but it will involve some serious planning with a calendar in hand. Again, it is not going to take many weeks, months, years of neglect before your wife, your husband, your children know who or what really counts, just how important they really are in the scheme of things! And, at that moment, when years later, you finally realize just how important your family really was, it is usually far too late having already left them behind to "get ahead"![7]

---

[7]David Elkind, *The Hurried Child: Growing Up Too Fast Too Soon* (Reading, MA: Addison-Wesley Publishing Co., 1981), believes today's

Parenting: Some Practical Suggestions

It is important to add here: what our children really need is *us*, not material possessions. (More on this later.) What an incredible tragedy if we think we must "get ahead" in our jobs, so that we can make more money, so that we can provide the material "things" that we — or they — think our family needs. Please don't make the mistake of justifying your "need" for professional advancement at their expense, or to justify your "need" for money and status by telling yourself you are giving them what they want! What they *really need is you, your* love, *your* presence, a real part of *your essence*, not more and more toys, etc. Someday they will thank you for giving them what they really needed and you won't have to wait all that long for the "thank you" either! If you want your child to grow up just like you, make sure you are worth being like! If on the other hand you don't want your child to grow up just like you — then it is even more important that you be worth being like. Think about it!

No "magic" number — nor an attempt at biblical numeration — is intended in our "twelve" suggestions. We are sure there are many, many more suggestions that could be given. These are some we have found useful in our family and in ministering to thousands over the years.[8]

---

young are "hurried children" who feel an intense pressure to achieve and a corresponding fear of failure. An urgent plea not to push them too hard!

[8]Dean & Grace Merrill, *Together at Home: 100 Proven Ways to Nurture Your Child's Faith* (Nashville: Thomas Nelson, 1985) is said to provide a refreshing alternative to sitting around the TV set.

CHAPTER EIGHT
Nurturing Children in the Lord

Before a family can minister as a family the "stage" has to be "set." There must be some understanding of what parenting is all about, especially for the Christian, and what is involved in preparing the family to minister. It is unfortunately our experience, that most children grow up in spite of their parents, not because of their help and guidance.[1] There is only one "most effective" way to nurture children in the Lord. *You must model what you are to them.* Or, perhaps, more accurately put: Like it or not, we always *do* in truth model what we are to them! Clearly, if we are to truly nurture children "in the Lord," we must model the love and character of God to our children. We have already talked some about this.

Many of us have heard someone mouth, "Train up a child in the way he should go and he will not depart from it." Proverbs 22:6 actually reads, "Train up a child in the way he should go, Even when he is old he will not depart from it." Often this is "quoted" by a parent almost in tears — in *great* agony — who has also just said something like, "How could this have happened? We didn't

---

[1] Orley Herron, *Who Controls Your Child?* (Nashville: Thomas Nelson, 1980) is considered a "must for all parents" by some Christian authorities. Michael Phillips, *Building Respect, Responsibility and Spiritual Values in Your Child* (Minneapolis: Bethany House, 1981) deals with the importance of an appropriate sense of esteem, instilling of spiritual values, and developing appropriate attitudes. Richard L. Strauss, *Confident Children and How They Grow* (Wheaton, IL: Tyndale, 1975) contains practical messages based on Scripture.

raise our child that way." "Raise your child what way?" comes the reply. "You know what we mean. We didn't raise our child to lie, cheat, or steal. We raised our children to be Christians. How could this have happened?" It is true that, "Virtue is harder to be got than knowledge of the world; and, if lost in a young man, is seldom [at least hard to be] recovered."[2]

Herein lies the question, "What is it to raise children to be Christians?" Does this mean to raise your child in a cold, rigid, legalistic system (home) like Terry's Th.D. colleague (mentioned in the last chapter) did?[3] We think not! In the many years since, Terry has often reflected about that man and his life. In all probability that man sincerely thought he was raising his children "in a Christian environment." However, we knew that family years later as the children grew up and all of his children had severe emotional and psychological problems that almost destroyed at least one of them. As our son, John, reminded us:

> All [this man's] children definitely had problems with social adaptation. They couldn't "think for themselves" and consequently, even though the children themselves "hated it," they became like "drones" or "robots" parroting standards and beliefs; again, which they didn't really agree with, but that

---

[2] Locke, *Some Thoughts On Education* (1693), Sec. 64.

[3] We are reminded of a most important statement Mark Berrier makes in *The Bible for Busy People*, "A Warning to the Reader: There is one thing you *must* avoid. You should not trust any group who believes that they alone have the truth. Any group who listens to only one leader or teacher, or any group who claims to be the only "true church," is dangerous. This is one of the marks of a *cult* — a group of people who allow no individual thinking, no freedom, and no differences of opinion. Avoid such groups. Instead, listen to more than one teacher; read everything you can. Then make your own decision to commit your life to Christ, totally. . . . And always test what you hear, comparing it to what the Bible actually says." p. ix. AN IMPORTANT WARNING!

Nurturing Children in the Lord

had been programmed into them by [their parent]. Consequently, they were often ostracized by even their Christian peers.

Raising children with "unrealistic demands," with "dead legalisms," or "rote mechanistic prayers" is NOT rearing them to be Christian! It is doing just the opposite! Again, as John said, "Eventually in 'breaking free' often these same children reject the faith and get 'caught up' in many of society's evils."[4] Raising children with "good intentions," loosely telling ourselves, "Oh, sure we are Christians," but never really modeling what it is to be "Christlike" for our children, is not raising them as Christians.

We are raising children to be Christian when we give them tender love and security, when we build in them a good self-image, when we provide a home in which they get to know and have a real relationship with the living, loving Lord Jesus. Our goal is to put them in the presence of Jesus! Could this be any clearer? Can we do this if *we* are not truly in His presence? Can we put our children in His presence when *we* are so busy working, playing, fighting, etc., that *we* don't have time for Him, or for them?

So many people and families have a "fun and games" approach to the Christian faith and to the church. They want a rich spiritual reward without the essential investment of a disciplined effort in Bible study, worship, giving, and fellowship. *Face it, Christians who spend only one or two hours a week in Bible study are not very serious about their faith*! Not just giving, but sacrificial giving is the heart of the Christian life — giving of time, talents, tithe, yes of our totality (Phil. 4:18-19). Surely all this must begin in the home.

---

[4]Phone conversation with John Hayden Miethe, 22 March 1995. John "worked" with three children from this family.

Duties of Parenthood

The Bible is *amazingly clear* about so many things. Recollect Mark Twain's comment? He was bothered by the parts of the Bible he *did* understand. If most of us want a starting place, it would be to practice the parts of the Bible we understand. Isaiah 38:18-19 says:

> For the grave cannot praise you, death cannot sing your praise; those who go down to the pit cannot hope for your faithfulness. The living, the living — they praise you, as I am doing today; *fathers tell their children about your faithfulness* (NIV, emphasis added).

Pretty clear, isn't it! FATHERS, TELL YOUR CHILDREN ABOUT YOUR FAITH![5] Whatever it means to "nurture" (and we will talk about this), it cannot be done effectively in the Christian context without the abiding presence of God in your life, as an individual and as a parent.

The Scriptures teach that parents have at least six special duties when it comes to their children:

(1) Parents have a duty "to teach" — and with diligence. Again, Deuteronomy 6:7! "Teach them diligently" about God! However, you cannot teach what you do not know. You have a clear obligation before the Lord to teach your children about God. This does not mean paying someone else to do it for you. It means that *you* teach your child what is important and why. Deuteronomy 6:20:

---

[5]Marshall L. Hamilton, *Father's Influence on Children* (Chicago: Nelson-Hall, 1977), provides more than analysis of statistics, how a father may increase his effectiveness, stimulating. Paul Heiderbrecht, *Fathering a Son* (Chicago: Moody Press, 1979). D. Bruce Lockerbie, *Fatherlove: Learning to Give the Best You've Got* (Garden City, NY: Doubleday, 1981). Gordon MacDonald, *The Effective Father* (Wheaton, IL: Tyndale House Publishers, 1977). Charlie W. Shedd, *Letters to Philip: On How to Treat a Woman* (Old Tappan, NJ: Fleming H. Revell Co., 1968).

> When your son asks you in time to come, saying, "What *do* the testimonies and the statutes and the judgments *mean* which the Lord our God commanded you?" then you shall say to your son . . . .

In the Christian context, we must teach our children about Jesus and especially the New Testament. We must teach them to *understand* what it says and why it is important to live our faith.

(2) Parents have a charge "to train" (Ps. 22:6). What is it to "train" a child? It is more than just abstract teaching by rote memory. "Training" involves an ordered sequence. "Training" sometimes has a negative connotation, but doesn't need to have. It involves all the military does to "equip" soldiers to know not just what their job is, but how to actually protect us. A special education teacher "trains" a child how to compensate for his or her learning disability. It is more than telling, it is showing. It is more than showing, it is involving! Beverly can't just tell them, or show them, but must *involve* them in the learning process. Get them to experience firsthand the concept. Many years ago, an elder in one of the churches we served gave Terry a plaque on which he had carved, "Tell me and I will forget, show me and I might remember, involve me and I will understand."[6] This is training and as parents we are responsible for all three aspects of

---

[6]On the back of the board was written, "Terry. This slogan is one used by the Oregon College of Education [now Western Oregon State College] at Monmouth, Oregon, a school founded in the 1850s [1856] as a frontier college by two of the sons of Alexander Campbell. As the private schools foundered in the late decades of the century the state assumed ownership and the school continues as one of three in Oregon's teacher training system. The central structure on campus is still known as Campbell Hall. Their other slogan is 'He who would teach must never cease to learn.' Thought this might decorate one of your classrooms. Sam."

it. Actually, this is really synonymous with teaching them to minister.

(3) Parents have a duty "to provide for." In some ways, for most of us this should be the most obvious, and possibly easiest, responsibility of parenthood. Paul says, by way of analogy, "After all, children should not have to save up for their parents, but parents for their children" (2 Cor. 12:14, NIV). We are to provide for our children's physical needs — safety, shelter, sustenance, shirts (clothing), etc. But so often we think we are "providing" for them when we are constantly buying this toy or that one because *they* think they "must have it." Actually, when we do this kind of "providing" — an overemphasis on material things — we are undercutting all our other parental responsibilities!

Yes, we bought our beloved son some nice toys, to be sure. But one of the "toys" he seemed to enjoy most and that stands out in memory was a little different than yesterday's Power Rangers. For the first five years or so of our married lives, Beverly had to go to a laundromat to do the washing because we were too poor to buy a washing machine. Finally, when we moved to St. Louis, we bought such a wonderful machine — wonderful to Beverly *and* to John Hayden. You see, he loved to play in the cardboard box the washing machine came in, and for months and months he did. After Terry cut "windows" and a "door" into the box, he would decorate it, color it, paint it, and most importantly pretend in it. He got more out of that "toy" he never knew he needed than all the ones he thought he did.

(4) Parents have a obligation "to nurture." In a real sense this whole chapter is about "nurturing" — at least nurturing children in the Lord. To "nurture" is the act of promoting development or growth; upbringing, rearing. In our experience, this may well be one of the most used "words" and, yet, most ignored concepts or "actions" in

our country today. If teaching entails "knowing" and "telling"; and, if training entails these as well as "showing" and "involving"; then, "nurturing" includes all of these plus "sustaining" and "growing." We do not "nurture" just by "teaching," or by "training," or "by providing for" physical needs. We nurture when we *support growth*, when we *build self-image*, when we *temper the spirit*, when we *expand horizons*, when we *gently and lovingly fashion our children into our adult Christian brothers and sisters*! Please reflect carefully on that last sentence.

(5) Parents have a duty "to control." Boy, that sounds negative, doesn't it? But should it? Many of us were "sold a bill of goods" when we were told that it stifled "creativity" to put behavioral limits on our children (and, perhaps, Dr. Spock was given "a bad rap" for supposedly teaching this). So these promoters of "laissez-faire" child rearing say, "The creative process needs freedom. If we set rules (establish behavioral conditions), then we harm the mental and social development of our children." NOT SO! Hardly anything could be further from the truth. This is *exactly* how we ended up with a large number of permissive, spoiled, insensitive brats. This "laissez-faire" child rearing is ultimately self-destructive! Almost, but not quite, exactly the opposite is the best method. "Freedom" must always be limited. Even ours as parents! "Creativity" demands structure, not sloppy "dilettantism" or spoiled arrogance! The issue is not "to control or not to control," but how much and when?

The "other side of the coin" is that parents as "control-freaks," as we have indicated, usually end up destroying their children. Sometimes the line is a fine one indeed between exerting proper control and just making the situation worse. If we have provided all the other aspects of the duty of parenthood — the responsibility of parents — as our children grew, then we will be able to quite naturally "loosen" the controls as they mature. In our family

Serving Christ: A Family Affair

it wasn't that hard really. From "day one" our son knew the commitments and "rules" of the household. He knew these were not optional; they were an important part of our self-identity as a family, and as individuals within that family. These became such a natural part of his life that as he grew older we had the wonderful freedom to not have to set down a whole encyclopedia of rules.

Just the other day, when we were talking to John Hayden and Nicole, John reminded us that he never really had a "curfew" as such. Does that mean that we were terribly lax parents? Hardly. He knew it wasn't appropriate to "run around" on a school night so that never became an issue. He knew we expected him home at a "decent" time on weekends. Besides (as he reminded us) most, if not all, the girls he dated had weekend curfews set by *their* parents (what other kind would he date?). If for any reason, he found that he was going to be later than 11:30 or midnight, he would always call us to tell us where he was and why he would be later than normal. He had learned to trust us and that we would always be there for him. We trusted him and grew to trust him more!

If you can believe it, John's practice of calling home if he was going to be out extra late continued well into college — though he was never asked to do so — during the times our son was actually living at home. Terry eventually wasn't terribly happy to be awakened after midnight by a 20-plus-year-old telling us that he and David had decided to take in a late movie and he would be home around such and such. [Terry really didn't mind.] The point is this: John Hayden had learned to be a considerate human being! He cared about his father and mother and wanted to be courteous enough to not cause them to worry unnecessarily.

Now you say, "Boy, you had it good, easy as parents!" Yes, we did! We also had some trying times. Everyone does. But the "easiness" of our way was because we loved and nurtured our son from the day he was born. Both of us, in the context of our friendships and ministries, have also had other experiences. When we were a fairly young married couple, two of our dearest friends (also a ministerial couple) had a daughter just a few years younger than our son. By the time this girl was three she had her parents wrapped totally around her finger! There was absolutely no question who ruled the roost in that family. But our dear friends evidently just couldn't see it!

We remember vividly many examples over the years of children gone wild. One over 20 years ago, when the parents of a college student of Terry's called us (more than once) in the middle of the night to drive to their town late at night/early in the morning to help with a crisis involving their teenage daughter. We tried and tried, but eventually she had to be put into the care of the authorities for her own protection. None of us liked this at all. But there simply was no other choice. Today, you hear the phrase "tough love" which means that sometimes you have to do what appears to be "a very unloving" thing because of real love.

There are a couple of things we want to say about this. (a) It is sometimes very difficult, and sometimes too late, for the parents to "undo" the damage that has already been done because a proper foundation was never really laid in the first place. This is why we emphasize throughout this book to start building your Christian home absolutely as early as possible. You should ideally start to build your Christian home before you even marry. As you recall, we also learn what something is by sometimes first learning what it is not! Even if you didn't come from a Christian home, you really learned more than you realize about "what not to do" as well as "what to do." *The "trick" is to recognize the psychological aspects of the negative behavior, reinforced by your home environment as you grew up, before it destroys your new home.*

Serving Christ: A Family Affair

We all have what we call "trigger mechanisms" — or in today's parlance "hot buttons." These are ingrained responses we learned in childhood with regard to how we respond to stress, tension, anger, etc., in the family. As we mature, we must be able to mentally see through these emotional triggers and deal with them. The only way this can be done is to first recognize them for what they are; and second, to get them out in the open, to discuss them with your spouse, so that each of you can be more aware of what is happening, and then begin to substitute new *learned responses* — positive "triggers" (if you like) — to take their place.

(b) Often, we simply need outside help to work through even the most sensitive family problem. The parent who is "becoming wiser" need not feel ashamed or embarrassed about the need for help. These parents realize that the truly wise thing to do is to seek the help needed *before it is too late*! As ministers and parents, we can tell you that we are indeed thankful there were others who could do for our family what we sometimes could not because we were too close to a particular situation. Thank God for His church, for the family of God!

(6) Parents have a trust "to love." There is so much that could be said about parental love. The *real* love, compassion, support, encouragement, and forgiveness of a parent lives on in the child long after the parent is gone. This true love becomes the foundation of the all-important self-image of the child. Ralph Waldo Emerson (1803-1882) once said of friendship that the glory of it is:

> . . . not the outstretched hand, nor the kindly smile nor the joy of companionship; *it is the spiritual inspiration that comes to one when he discovers that someone else believes in him and is willing to trust him* [emphasis added].

Now to be sure, parents cannot "afford the luxury" of

just being "friends" to their children. In other words, parenting demands so much more than friendship. Your children need friends, but *when they are children they need you to be parents*. When they become adults and have families of their own, then *they need you to be friends*, in a true way, which does not interfere and is not judgmental. Surely this "spiritual inspiration" Emerson refers to is something we, as parents, must strive to give our children. For them to know that we love them is to know that we believe in them and trust them. Love is not an emotion; it is a way of life.

Discipline and Punishment are NOT the Same

The older we get and the more we experience, the more we are convinced that one of the real problems in many homes is a lack of knowledge of, and skills in, parenting! So often we see parents confuse discipline with punishment. *"Punishment" is what must be used when "discipline" fails.* By now we have said this several times. Yet it bears repeating because there is a tremendous misunderstanding here.

An experience we had lately illustrates the confusion handily. On one of the most famous nationally televised talk shows, we happened to see a segment about families and family "discipline." Three or four families were represented. One of the families talked on and on about how they had to "whip their children with a stick and send them to bed afterwards at least four or five nights a week." First, it doesn't take a genius — that "rocket scientist" — to see something is terribly wrong in that family. Second, it should be obvious that if the parents have to resort to whipping their children practically every night of the week, what they called "discipline" or "punishment" — for this family certainly the same thing — was *failing miserably*! Further, one has to wonder if what was

Serving Christ: A Family Affair

going on was not actually abuse and physical cruelty.[7]

But as terrible as this part of the story is, what we have just related is not perchance the worst aspect of it. When the other families on the show challenged the father and mother, who meted out corporal punishment with a stick night after night, as to whether they were doing the correct thing, the parents who whipped their children were adamant — unyielding, uncompromising; even angry — and insisted they were doing this because they were Christians! They proceeded to quote (to misquote and take out of context) Scripture to justify their parental "discipline." "Spare the rod and spoil the child!" they said.[8]

But what about Scriptures like, "O Lord, do not rebuke me in Thine anger, nor chasten me in Thy wrath [anger]"(Ps. 6:1). Surely, it is "common sense" that if we have a right to expect, or even ask, our Heavenly Father not to rebuke or chasten us in His wrath, we as parents should not do so to our children either! Or, ". . . do not provoke your children to anger; but bring them up in the *discipline* and instruction of the Lord" (Eph. 6:4). Again, "discipline" is not punishment. In fact, here we see another excellent basis for "discipline," that is Christian *education*! We were also saddened that the family which confused extreme corporal punishment with discipline was the only family on the show that identified themselves as "Christian."

Remember: you will probably get out of your child what they see in you and just about what you really expect from them! So many parents sell their children short. The children see the hypocrisy and know if you don't really care.

---

[7]See chapter 7, "Parenting: Some Practical Suggestions," suggestion one, pp. 111-112.

[8]Perhaps having Scriptures in mind like Proverbs 13:24, "He who spares his rod hates his son," as well as Proverbs 19:18; 22:15; 23:13-14; 29:15, 17.

What is "Nurturing Children in the Lord"?

Actually, we have already said much in the book about "nurture." We will give some specific ideas about "The Family and Ministry" in chapter 11. It should be clear by this point in the book that in a very real sense "ministry" must be a natural outgrowth of the commitments and priorities of the family. If the family is truly a loving committed Christian family, then they are probably ministering in a number of ways already, even though they may not always think of it "as service" or realize overtly what is going on.

We believe that helping children mature is a sober business to be taken most seriously, and worked at daily. Our whole contention here is that if children are truly "nurtured" in the Lord they will "radiate" Christian love and ministry as naturally as the *new* nature they have in Christ, a nature they undoubtedly saw modeled in you as parents! We have pointed out that nurturing is more than teaching. We said it involved:

(1) Promoting development, upbringing, rearing. By "upbringing," we certainly do not mean teaching them to be "class conscious." "Class" consciousness has no place in the heart of the Christian. "Arrogance" in any form is anti-Christian. We used words like "sustaining" and "growing." In general, perhaps, the most important, and most difficult, aspect of being a parent is the attempt at constantly being that stable support, that bridge over troubled water, that gentle "encourager" (but not pusher) in the life of a child. This one gets harder as they grow. Often, you have to be that incredible support right beside them without being "right beside" them. But the more they have grown to trust you, and the more they mature and you grow to trust them, the more you and your strength *is* right beside them even when you must "hold back."

Essentially, this "growth" which we must support in

Serving Christ: A Family Affair

each child is the same growth that the Scriptures tell us Jesus Himself experienced. Luke 2:40 says the "Child continued to grow and become strong, increasing in wisdom; and the grace of God was upon Him." In 2:52 we read, ". . . Jesus kept increasing in wisdom and stature, and in favor with God and men." We nurture when we support growth in every way possible. Obviously, this growth in the Christian context involves every aspect of maturing in our understanding of God, who Jesus is, the role and function of the Holy Spirit in our lives, and what it is to live what we claim to believe.

(2) Building a good self-image. This is another hard, but most essential aspect of parenting! It would be hard indeed to say too much about the importance of this responsibility![9] As we have pointed out, you certainly do not build a good self-image by constantly beating a child down psychologically or physically. If, in our day, it seems like a rather incredible percentage of children are physically abused; then, just think of the number who are psychologically abused. Psychological abuse leaves the longest lasting scars! We have all too many examples of children as young as seven years old who have committed murder. You ask how those so young could do such a hideous thing. Why shouldn't they, when life means nothing to them? When their lives have no meaning!

You know, there are a lot of ideas "out there" which seem silly, absurd really, when you look carefully at what is being promoted. Two quick examples will serve to illustrate: (1) In philosophy with regard to the debate over "free will" versus "determinism,"[10] one scholar has said so well, "In essence determinism is one of those theories which . . . are so preposterously silly that only very

---

[9] See pp. 55, 121-122, 129, 155, 158 of this book.

[10] The belief that everything we do or will do is actually predetermined in every case.

Nurturing Children in the Lord

learned men could have thought of them."[11] (2) In the creation / evolution debate, two scientists calculate the chances of life arising spontaneously, even if the whole universe were a kind of prebiotic soup, would be 1 in 10 with 40,000 zeros written after. The scientists compare this with the chances of a Boeing 747 resulting from a tornado raging through a junkyard.[12]

What does this have to do with our responsibility as parents to "build good self-images" in our children? How could we, as parents, be so "preposterously silly" as to think that something as fragile, as complex, as important as a child's self-worth could just happen on its own without a great deal of warm loving nurture? And, yet, many of us go through our children's lives never giving much of a thought — let alone action — to what we are doing to their view of themselves by *our actions* or lack of them. It has been shown over and over again that a person will not value others if one believes one has no value as an individual.

My wife is an exceptional teacher! She makes her job much more work than is necessary to "do the job." Many years ago, Beverly started doing everything she could in the classroom to reinforce positive behavior and to reward success — not to belittle children because of their failures, as many of us have experienced even in high school and college. For example, Beverly marks what is correct on a paper, not what is wrong. Granted it takes much more time to do it this way, but think of the subtle positive reinforcement. Rather than always emphasizing the incorrect, do it in the context of praise. You will get amazing results, really!

Yes, there must be limits — and punishments when limits are crossed. But every time you can praise your

---

[11]Miethe, *Living Your Faith*, p. 50.

[12]Miethe & Habermas, *Why Believe? God Exists!*, p. 80. See Miethe & Flew, *Does God Exist? A Believer*, 1991.

Serving Christ: A Family Affair

child for doing something, encourage them in trying something new and difficult, and praise them in their effort no matter how "good" or "bad" they were, you lay a brick in the wall of a good self-image. A child is in many ways a fragile being, and perhaps the most fragile part is the "ego." The truth of the matter is that given the way most children are raised it is a miracle of the Holy Spirit that we don't have higher, much higher divorce and/or murder rates than we do. Think about it. (Recall the material, "9. Build a good self-image in your child" in chapter 7.)

(3) Temper the spirit. "Temper" is a marvelous word. To "temper" is "to modify by the addition of some moderating agent or quality," to harden, strengthen, or toughen. In music to "temper" is to adjust or to tune. It also refers to a state of mind or emotions, mood or disposition.[13] When we temper the spirit, we set about to help make the "psyche" or consciousness of a person more Christlike. This, of course, must be done by word and by example.

For the Christian, that "moderating agent" which helps to strengthen the process should involve at least three aspects: (a) The Scriptures. Psalm 119:9-11 again comes to mind. By "hiding" the word of God in our hearts, we begin to get the "raw material" needed to temper the spirit! "Thy word I have treasured in my heart, That I may not sin against Thee." (b) The Holy Spirit. "You, however, are controlled not by the sinful nature but by the Spirit, if the Spirit of God lives in you . . ." (Rom. 8:9, NIV; see also John 14:17; 15:26; 16:13). The Holy Spirit speaks through the Scriptures in the life of the

---

[13]In Greek thought a middle course, a compromise between extremes. According to medieval physiology, the character or constitution of a man as determined by the mixture within him of the four humors.

believer. We must stop taking the presence of the Holy Spirit for granted in life.

And (c) the prayers and actions of parents. As parents, we have the incredible responsibility and great privilege, of helping mold our children into brothers and sisters in the Lord! It is the parents, after all, who have the chief responsibility to educate their children in general and to bring their children into the presence of the Lord. If we give up this responsibility, we have all but abdicated our "parenthood." As parents, we can model and mold our children so that they are "strengthened," "toughened," "tuned" in to the Lord — so that their attitudes, emotions, moods, and actions develop in a Christlike manner. This is a day by day, year by year process which we must engage in with prayer, patience, and the presence of the Holy Spirit.

(4) Expanding horizons. If, in this day and age, we need the church to "get out of the box," how much more do we as parents have a responsibility to "keep current" at least with regard to our children's world (the world of tomorrow) if we are really to be a force in expanding their horizons. The term says much. "Expanding horizons" means simply to help teach them how to "see beyond," to *look ahead*, to *anticipate*, to be *responsible* for their actions. Simply said, but *not* simply done. *We* need to see life as "a great adventure" so *they* can appreciate, prepare for, and survive their "adventure." "Positive thinking" may not always be *the* answer, but it sure beats the opposite extreme. If you are one who seems almost always to take a negative, dark view of life; why then, pray tell, would you be surprised when your children seem to be "born" pessimists? Help your child grow by expanding horizons in order to "see beyond."

(5) Gently and lovingly fashioning our children into our adult Christian equals, peers before the Lord. This should be the goal of every Christian parent! Contrary to

Serving Christ: A Family Affair

what some teach, the "eternal" relationship is not that of parent / child, but of brother and sister in Christ, joint heirs in the Kingdom of God.[14] When it is all said and done, our chief responsibility as parents is to teach, to mold our children so that one day we and they will be equals in the Lord — brothers and sisters in Christ! This is the chief role of parenting and greatest joy of being parents. Can there really be a more challenging or exciting "job" in life than that of "nurturing children in the Lord" and of living to share as adults the fullness of life in Christ?

---

[14]See p. 46 of this book.

CHAPTER NINE

The Family that Prays *and* Plays Together

Do you recall the old slogan often seen on bus stop benches, and on the buses themselves, "The family that prays together stays together"? We do. In fact, last semester Terry taught a philosophy class on ethics at a local college and on the cover of one of the textbooks was a picture with a collage filling up the figure of a cross. One of the pictures in the collage was of a billboard in Hollywood announcing a "crusade for family prayer" and that, "God makes house calls. The family that prays together stays together."[1] Yes, this is a "truism," but one which paints a beautiful and powerful picture. Prayer is important to the family!

The purpose of this chapter is not to give an "exhaustive" study of the doctrine of prayer, but to talk more specifically about the importance of prayer and unity to the family.[2] We will address some "hindrances" to and

---

[1] The text was: Paul T. Jersild & Dale A. Johnson, editors, *Moral Issues & Christian Response*, Fifth edition (New York: Harcourt Brace College Publishers, 1993), p. 39.

[2] For some helpful material on prayer see: Miethe, "On Prayer" in *The New Christian's Guide to Following Jesus*, pp. 85-90; *Beginning Your New Life in Prayer* (San Bernardino, CA: Here's Life Publishers, Inc.); Elinore Mapes Pierce, *The Prayers of the Bible* (Philadelphia: The Judson Press, 1944); John Guest, *Only a Prayer Away: Finding Deeper Intimacy with God* (Ann Arbor, MI: Servant Publications, 1985); William Law, *The Spirit of Prayer,* [and] *The Spirit of Love*. Edited by Sidney Spencer (Cambridge: James Clarke, 1969); Herbert Lockyer, *The Power of Prayer* (Nashville: Thomas Nelson, 1982); Curtis G. Mitchell, *Praying Jesus' Way: A New Approach to Personal Prayer* (Old Tappan, NJ: Fleming H. Revell Co., 1977); Andrew Murray, *The Believer's School of Prayer*

Serving Christ: A Family Affair

"aids" for prayer. *A family really does need to pray to thrive.* But this prayer must be more than just the traditional bowing of the head before meals or as a part of a specific worship activity. Prayer in the family must be seen as a natural communication with God, as a natural part of family life. More than a "spirit of unity" in any family, we should seek a unity of Spirit!

Many of us are afraid of a "regular prayer time" or regular "grace" said before meals. Afraid it will become a time of "dull rote" recitations and oft-repeated phrases. In one family we know quite well, "grace" was always said before meals, but the "prayer" was almost always the same and the TV was always blaring in the background. It was hard to take it seriously or to concentrate on what was being said. In a church we were members of in high school, many of the elders would say exactly the same prayer — word for word — at the communion table every single time. You can imagine the effect on the people of the congregation, but evidently the elder(s) couldn't.

When we practice this kind of "dull" and "rote" prayer, we are teaching our children something very bad, and may actually be destroying their future prayer lives in the bargain! But this need not be.

> The anxiety is quite unfounded, that a regular participation in family prayer, and in grace at mealtime, will become a dead mechanism. If in the parents there be true faith, devotion, and a higher sanctification, this "danger" falls to the ground; but if these qualities be lacking in the parents, then their attempts at religious influence are all in vain. Those

---

(Minneapolis: Bethany House, 1982); Warren & Ruth Myers, *Pray: How to Be Effective in Prayer* (Colorado Springs: NavPress, 1983); Ray C. Stedman, *Talking to My Father: What Jesus Teaches About Prayer* (Portland, OR: Multnomah Press, 1984); Lance Webb, *The Art of Personal Prayer* (Nashville: Abingdon Press, 1962); Charles Francis Whiston, *Teach Us To Pray: A Study of Distinctively Christian Praying* (Boston: The Pilgrim Press, 1949).

The Family That Prays and Plays Together

who allow so much anxiety, lest the child's prayer should become a spiritless mechanism, should see whether their own prayer, if they are accustomed to pray at all, be not such.[3]

Again, the responsibility — at least initially — falls squarely on the shoulders of the parents. If prayer is basically a conversation with God, do we always say the exact same thing to anyone else when we talk to them?

We are worried by the way some of the college students we know pray. We hear an increasing tendency to pray in a certain way. It seems that someone is teaching — we are sure by example — many of them to think "effective" or "sincere" prayer is something you say as rapidly as possible with as little "obvious" thought as possible. This "machine-gun" approach to prayer is seasoned with the word "Lord" or "Father" sprinkled in as often as possible. Some of these students even add to this a louder voice, etc., when praying. Remember, if sincerity is not a test for truth, neither is it necessarily a test for effective prayer. There is no substitute for careful thought in prayer; and, sometimes the less said the better. We must stop praying in gross generalities and start praying for specific people, specific needs, specific things for which we are thankful. We need not try to "cover the universe" in one prayer.

"Topics" and "Types" of Prayer

As testified to above, family prayers must be kept alive by making sure they address issues of current importance to the family and beyond. "Variety" in prayer helps keep it from becoming a "dead mechanism." In the beginning, to aid family members with ideas and topics, it might be helpful to choose a daily general area or topic on which

---

[3]Christenson, *The Christian Family*, 174.

Serving Christ: A Family Affair

to concentrate your prayers. Examples: Mondays might be for prayers for individual family members; Tuesdays, prayers for missionaries; Wednesdays, for the nation; Thursdays, for neighbors and friends; Fridays, for peace; Saturdays, prayers for the church, etc. But pick and choose topics that have special meaning for your family.

It would also be helpful for family members to distinguish between different types of prayer by picking different topics to emphasize for the day or week. For instance, some Christian thinkers say a "prayer of faith" has as its objective getting a job done. There are also "prayers of confession" or "intercession" (entreaty in favor of another) — to ask God to act, say, in an individual's life in a certain way. C.R. Findley relates an interesting example:

> Answers to prayer often come in unexpected ways. We pray, for instance, for a certain virtue; but God seldom delivers Christian virtues all wrapped in a package and ready for use. *Rather he puts us in situations where by his help we can develop those virtues.* Henry Ward Beecher told of a woman who prayed for patience, and God sent her a poor cook. The best answers to prayer may be the vision and strength to meet a circumstance or to assume a responsibility [emphasis added].

There are also prayers of "thanksgiving"; of "praise" or "adoration"; of "meditation"; etc.[4]

When you don't have time to take a half-hour, some people call a quick prayer in the middle of a day at work

---

[4]Meditation is a much neglected form of prayer which has been highly cultivated in the Eastern Orthodox Church. It is a quiet prayer intended to help place you deeply in the presence of God. Anselm of Canterbury (1033-1109) developed the Ontological Argument for the existence of God one day while meditating in prayer in his garden on the concept of an absolutely perfect Being. See Miethe & Habermas, *Why Believe? God Exists!*, pp. 65-71; Miethe & Flew, *Does God Exist?*, pp. 150, 178-181.

an "Arrow Prayer." "You pray right now because a situation has come up." Or, perhaps, it is a quick prayer for strength at a particularly demanding time, or a special immediate feeling of thankfulness. Christenson says, "Of course, arrow prayers are only successful, as a general rule, when they are well grounded in the life of prayer." That be as it may, certainly such prayers will be much more likely to be "effective" as part of an ongoing prayer life. "People who live out of their pockets don't have an adequate diet. Neither do people find the power of God filling their prayers who try to exist spiritually on moments of prayer fleetingly flung toward heaven."[5]

Apart from a "bolt of lightning" from Heaven in answer, prayer can and should have a calming presence in the life of the believer. It can be a tranquil reassurance of the moment by moment presence of God. It can help set the whole mental attitude in the most positive way during a time of potential conflict or stress. In fact, we need to rediscover prayer as a part of Christian meditation.[6] At the very least, it is a powerful way to emphasize and to commemorate the presence of God right here, right now. It is hard to overemphasize the importance of such a realization, such a feeling.

The Parent-Priest and Prayer

The "parent-priest" — what a beautiful and biblical concept! Just as *every Christian* should see himself or herself as a minister of Christ; even more should every parent see himself or herself as a parent-minister to their family. The parent-priest has a truly wonderful, and very serious responsibility, to (1) present each child before God, to (2) intercede on each child's behalf before the

---

[5]Christenson, *The Christian Family*, pp. 186, 188.
[6]Edmund Prosper Clowney, *CM: Christian Meditation* (Nutley, NJ: Craig Press, 1979).

Serving Christ: A Family Affair

Lord, and to (3) present the Lord to each child. What an incredible privilege, and great will be our accountability before the Lord! We need to be talking to God about our children frequently throughout the day. Nothing could be more essential than prayer to the office of this parent-parson.

There is also a powerful role for the Grandparent-priest. But we very quickly add, this role must by played without making demands on your grown children! Prayer is essential here as well. Terry told me recently that he prays even more regularly for John and his wife Nicole (our "daughter") now that they have a son. In fact, numerous times throughout the day, he prays for them all as naturally as he thinks about them. We know now some of what they have to look forward to and, as grandparents, are even more concerned that they understand the importance of the presence of Christ in their home.

Family prayer is not merely a beautiful human custom, it is "bedrock" of the Christian family. There are many, many things of value that we can — indeed, must — teach our children, but NONE is more important than teaching them to really pray, for thus we bring our child into intimate contact with their God. But, here again, we must bear in mind the importance of the developmental stages of a child's growth. We need to help our children learn to pray so they first understand the importance of prayer and then to understand that for which they are praying. The first of these can be taught to them at a very young age.

Prayer and the Will of the Father

The Christian's goal should be continually to learn more of God's will and to act on that knowledge. In Romans 2:17-24, Paul discusses the importance of attempting to live out God's will by bringing our will into line with His. Paul says the Jews are hypocrites: they teach God's will to others, but they do not live it themselves. Christians must be free from this, careful to put into practice what they study and learn about God's will from Scripture, "But prove yourselves doers of the word, and not merely hearers who delude themselves" (James 1:22).

Christians often expect God to supply them with a blueprint detailing every aspect of their lives. Not so! Yet there are two points of God's will which are the same for everyone: (1) His general will is that a person be saved, that is, live in relation to Him,[7] and (2) His specific will is that each person offer his or her talents and abilities to God, freely choosing the way to serve Him which will be most fruitful, given the needs of the time and the individual's abilities.

Consequently, a very important aspect of prayer is the thought, "Does this agree with the will of God?"[8] God simply doesn't contradict Himself. Normally, we are very thankful for this truth. But we need to remember that we can't twist God's arm to get Him to do something against His will. This should be very clearly and easily understood, but it isn't. Recall in the Lord's Prayer (Matt. 6:9-13), the model for prayer, Jesus told us to pray, "Thy will be done."

Often, we seem to think that simply tacking on at the

---

[7]See Miethe, "The Universal Power of the Atonement" in *The Grace of God, The Will of Man*, Edited by Clark H. Pinnock (Grand Rapids: Zondervan, 1989), pp. 71-96.

[8]See Miethe, "Ministry and the Christian" and "God and the Day's Work, in *The New Christian's Guide to Following Jesus*, pp. 103-110, 117-122. A couple of excellent resources with regard to the will of God in general: Paul E. Little, *Affirming the Will of God* (Downers Grove, IL: InterVarsity Press, 1971); and Garry Friesen, *Decision Making and the Will of God: A Biblical Alternative to the Traditional View* (Portland, OR: Multnomah Press, 1980), 452 pages. See also Leslie D. Weatherhead, *The Will of God* (Nashville: Abingdon, 1944).

Serving Christ: A Family Affair

end of our prayer "if it be Thy will" is enough. It isn't! We have a responsibility to try to discern the will of God by knowing and understanding Scripture. Again, "casual" Bible study just isn't enough. As we mature in the faith, we will learn to discern more readily what is God's will. First John 5:14 says, "And this is the confidence which we have before Him, that if we ask anything according to His will, He hears us."

Some Christians make a quite strong distinction between a prayer of "faith" and, say, a prayer for "guidance." "What if you don't know whether it is God's will? Then don't pray for it. If you don't know that something is God's will, you have no business praying for it. It would be better then to pray a prayer for guidance and determine what God's will is."[9] Terry likes Iñigo López de Loyola's famous prayer, "Teach us, good Lord, to serve Thee as Thou deservest: to give and not to count the cost; to fight and not heed the wounds; to toil and not to seek for rest; to labor and not to ask for any reward save that of knowing that we do Thy will."[10] God gives us his guidance in many ways: through the Bible, through a Christian spouse, Christian family, Christian friends, and sometimes through His church.

Prayer and "Personal" Choice

True, we need to listen carefully and attentively, but sometimes God wants us to make up our own minds with regard to more than one equally valid option. Sometimes our choice must be made in relation to the need at the time, our personal psychology, or how our immediate family fits into this or that act. Often, God has — or we have — already chosen priorities that need to be figured

---

[9]Christenson, *The Christian Family*, p. 181.
[10]Ignatius Loyola (1491-1556), *Prayer for Generosity* (1548).

into the decision. A prayer for guidance can also be a rather tricky thing. Sometimes we say we want God's guidance, but aren't really all that keen on accepting it when it comes. Just remember first of all that it isn't "guidance" from the Lord if it contradicts the teaching of Scripture.

On many, perhaps most, issues we have genuine choice! In these cases we must not make our choice on purely "emotional" grounds. For example, we have actually seen missionaries whip people up into an emotional frenzy when trying to get some in the audience to make a commitment to that particular missionary endeavor. And, as a result of psychological manipulation, individuals made a commitment they shouldn't have. We have known of more than a few cases where the mission, as well as the individual who made the commitment, would have been much better off if the individual had chosen otherwise. We have seen well-intentioned parents put such a "call to missions" — for which they were ill equipped — before their commitment to their six children. Consequently, the children suffered for the rest of their adult lives because of their parents' decision which should have been made with the needs of the whole family in mind, not just the "desires" of the parents.

If we are asking God for guidance with regard to some specific area in which we really do have a wide range of choices, it is best first of all to put the choice in the context of knowing and understanding the commitments we have already made, knowing our talents and skills as well as our limitations, and knowing our psychological makeup. *Sometimes we can have the best of intentions and make the worst of choices, especially if we make them in haste or without examining our previous commitments to God to see if there is a conflict!*

Serving Christ: A Family Affair

Hindrances to Prayer

It might be helpful to briefly address "hindrances" to prayer. There are many such hindrances:

(1) Resentment, or an unforgiving spirit. This is one of the most important and yet hardest lessons to learn in life — one that seems to have to be learned over and over again: Another person cannot rob you of your peace. *The only thing that can rob you of your peace is your attitude, or your sin.* Resentment only hurts the one doing the resenting! Do what you can to redeem the past, then give it over to God and forget it! Let God take care of it. This is not to say that it is wrong to feel sad or hurt. To do so is human and important in and of itself. But if you allow your "feelings" to dominate you, you are allowing someone else to control you. And, when someone or something else is controlling you, God cannot have His proper place in your thoughts and in your life.

(2) Sin. If there is a sin in your life, then take it to God in prayer believing that if you are genuinely sorry and repent, He will forgive! Psalm 66:16-20 says, in part:

> Come and hear, all who fear God, And I will tell of what He has done for my soul. . . . If I regard wickedness in my heart, The Lord will not hear; But certainly God has heard; He has given heed to the voice of my prayer. Blessed be God, Who has not turned away my prayer, Nor His lovingkindness from me.

In John 9:32, the man Jesus healed who was blind from birth says to the Pharisees, "We know that God does not listen to sinners. He listens to the godly man who does his will" (NIV).[11] James 5:16-20 tells us:

---

[11] This is an important prelude to the incredible discussion Jesus has with the Pharisees regarding "spiritual blindness" in John 9:35-10:21.

The Family That Prays and Plays Together

> . . . confess your sins to one another, and pray for one another, so that you may be healed. The effective prayer of a righteous man can accomplish much. . . . let him know that he who turns a sinner from the error of his way will save his soul from death and will cover a multitude of sins.

We *must* take everything to God in prayer! Sound familiar?

(3) Guilt. Guilt is a terribly debilitating thing and one of the most powerful tools Satan uses to defeat us. False guilt especially is one of the most EXHAUSTING problems in the Christian life. It is very hard indeed to live a life of vitality and energy when you are smothered with guilt. The *answer* to the problem of guilt, both real and imagined, is twofold: (a) Real repentance is required for forgiveness,[12] and (b) then we must actually accept that we are forgiven. Serious trust in the Lord is necessary to let guilt go! False guilt is actually a "slap in the face" of our Lord. Parents must not put false guilt on a child; nothing will destroy a self-image more quickly!

(4) Doubt. While "doubt" can play a quite positive role in rational inquiry, and can be a true friend of faith; it can be absolutely devastating to your prayer life. It is certainly true that the whole basis for prayer must be found in believing and trusting God and His Word. All our fears, doubts, the truly brutal events of our lives (often from childhood) are buried just under the surface. We must not let them rule us! Of course, this change will not occur overnight, but only through a process of re-education and good experiences — reaffirmation — to replace the old. This is where a fellow believer or a Christian spouse can be invaluable! We are so thankful for each other and that God "gave" John Hayden and

---

[12]Terry is currently working on a book entitled: *Making Forgiveness Real* to be available from College Press in the future.

Serving Christ: A Family Affair

Nicole to each other. Confidence, trust, and faith do not grow in a day.

Bear in mind, NO ONE deserves to be abused, belittled, beaten, or maligned through life as are so many children and spouses. If you came from such a home, then the very best thing you can do for yourself is to: (a) seek solid professional counseling to help you work through your past so that you can finally, truly let it go; (b) constantly tell yourself you are special, you are of infinite worth in God's eyes and you deserve to be treated as one created in the very image of God; and (c) put yourself in as positive a physical and emotional environment as possible! In this a good, supportive church should help. Get away from anyone who belittles you as fast as you can!

(5) Confusing God's timing with your desires. God's timing frequently is not our timing! *Waiting on God can be one of the most important lessons anyone can learn.* Just ask Job! One of the most important characteristics a parent can teach a child is "patience" or "serenity" — peace of mind. Reinhold Niebuhr's prayer has become one of the most famous in modern times: "O God, give us the serenity to accept what cannot be changed; courage to change what can be changed; and wisdom to distinguish one from the other."[13] It acknowledged three very important attitudes: The ability to endure, to live through, the painful in life; courage to act when action is warranted, reasonable; and the wisdom to know the fertile from the

---

[13] A prayer of Reinhold Niebuhr's (1892-1971) in 1934 composed when he preached, as he occasionally did, in the small church near his summer home in Heath, Massachusetts. After the service, a summer neighbor by the name of Howard Chandler Robbins asked for a copy. He is reported to have been handed the original, with words to the following effect, "Here, take the prayer. I have no further use for it." Robbins published it as part of a pamphlet in 1935. It has been adopted as the motto of Alcoholics Anonymous; the U.S.O. distributed millions of copies to servicemen during World War II.

futile. If, as parents, we could only instill such in our children, surely they would have peace of mind.

(6) The reality of Satan. We sometimes wonder, is it harder to believe in the power, reality, and presence of God, or in the presence of Satan? Those of us who know God, know that there is a real, personal, incredibly powerful presence of Evil. One of the biggest mistakes people make is to underestimate the power of the Evil One. We need to teach our children how to be strong against the attacks of this archfiend. Recollect Augustine's powerful insight we discussed in chapter one. It is Satan's place to get us to choose *Self* over God! (Luke 11:5-13, 18:1-8). The strength of the Holy Spirit and Christian discipline are the keys to defeating Beelzebub. In this fight, the Christian's most powerful weapon is prayer. Jesus went through "agony" in Luke 22:44 and Paul tells us to pray that way in Romans 15:30. If we study the meaning of "agony" for prayer we may learn how to use prayer skillfully. For a discussion of "'Agony': Key to Christian Victory" see Terry's *Living Your Faith*, pages 99-108.

Aids to Prayer

Yet prayer can be, and ought to be, a powerful tool in the believer's armory. We remember the beautiful story of Valiant in the *Pilgrims Progress*:

> "That was a hard battle, three men to one" said Greatheart. "Yes," replied Valiant; "but I knew I was fighting against my King's enemies, and that gave me courage." "Did you not cry for help? Some of the King's servants might have been near enough to hear you." "*I cried to the King Himself, and I am sure He answered me. I could not have fought so long in my own strength.*" Greatheart smiled, "You are one of our King's true servants! Let me see your sword. Ah, yes, this is from the right armory!" "It is a good sword,"

Serving Christ: A Family Affair

said Valiant. "No man who has so fine a weapon need be afraid, if he has learned how to use it skillfully" [emphasis added].[14]

We need to learn to "use" prayer skillfully.

(1) Start and end each day with prayer. We suggested this in chapter three (p. 57). "Habit" doesn't have to be a "dirty word." *It is hard to over stress the importance of establishing "workable" disciplines in your life and that of your family.* Herein is a key to Christian living. Søren Kierkegaard (1813-1855) once prayed, "Father in Heaven, when the thought of thee wakes in our hearts, let it not awaken like a frightened bird that flies about in dismay, but like a child waking from its sleep with a heavenly smile." Children who "sleep" in the Lord not only rest easy, but can awaken with a heavenly smile! Our son did. Our grandson does. As parents, we should do everything in our power to help our children know such peace.

It is very common, even in families that are only casually "religious" (rather than really Christian), to have the child say a prayer before bed. But in the Christian home, why not have the parent and child get down on their knees together for prayer. Parents, why not say a "brief" prayer of "blessing" — asking God to bless and keep your child day by day, and always (Mark 10:16) — and "thanksgiving" to God for the child. You say you want to build a good self-image in your child. What better way to start than with thanking God for them regularly in their presence! The earlier you begin praying for your child (in their presence) and with them the better. Why not start the day they are born and continue everyday they are in your care!

---

[14]Told in longer form in Miethe, *Living Your Faith*, 99-100. See Helen L. Taylor, *Little Pilgrim's Progress* [adapted from John Bunyan's (1628-1688) classic work] (Chicago: Moody Press, n.d.), pp. 236-237.

The Family That Prays and Plays Together

(2) Keep a "quiet time" each day.[15] A quite time can be a time for prayer, or meditation in general, or a time to reflect on a small portion of Scripture, or even a short passage from a devotional classic.[16] Such a time is best when the activity is varied on occasion so that all the above are done periodically. As indicated in the name, it should be a "quieting" time, a time to "center" your life and thoughts on God, on what is really important. It can help give meaning and balance to daily life. Some of us think the busier we get the less time we have for such a "luxury," but the truth is a "quiet time" is not a luxury and becomes even more important the more hectic our schedule. The earlier we teach our children to have such a personal time, the more they will experience its importance and the more it will become an essential part of their daily lives.

(3) Have a regular time for the family to pray together. At mealtime is fine, but we don't think family prayer should be restricted to those times. The best time for such family prayer may vary from season to season and as the family grows and matures. Generally, it is best to pick a period that is part of a larger block of "non-hectic" time in the daily progression of things. Again, as with anything, the modern family seems to be able to "carve out" time for almost anything any individual family member desires. So, why should it be so hard to find ten minutes or so for prayer which is so important to family life and growth?

---

[15] A time for peaceful, serene, tranquil, calm reflection.

[16] For example: William Law (1686-1761), *A Serious Call to the Devout and Holy Life* (London: A Hodder & Stoughton Christian Classic, 1987) originally published in 1729. Law described "stated hours of prayer" as: early morning for praise and thanksgiving, 9:00 for humility, 12:00 noon for universal love and intercession, 3:00 p.m. for surrender to God, 6:00 p.m. for confession and repentance, and bedtime for the certainty of death ("Introduction," p. x).

Serving Christ: A Family Affair

(4) Make prayer meaningful, real. *Whatever you do, pray.* Make sure you have time for prayer that has real meaning! It may be worse than "useless" to just "go through the motions" in that it sets a bad precedent for, and sends a bad message to, everyone involved, including God! We are not convinced that praying each day "six times a day" (though regularity of schedule is a great help in personal discipline), at exactly the same time is what is important here. But, whenever we pray, take time to "do it right." What is "doing it right?" Recall the father reading the newspaper when his child comes to him and says something of importance — to the child — and daddy responds, "Oh, yes" but basically ignores the child. A person praying must not be like that father. Consciousness, volition — an act of will — must be focused on God when we pray!

(5) Yet make it enjoyable, fun. We cannot emphasize too much that prayer — and almost every aspect of family life and ministry — can be "fun" (as well as serious) for the Christian family. God has a great sense of humor. After all, He created us, humankind, didn't He? "Serious" and "morbid" are not synonyms! There are different types of speech appropriate for different occasions; e.g., more formal or more casual. Different circumstances may lend themselves to different types of prayer. Prayer *is* basically a conversation with God and we should be able to be happy and joyous when we talk to God.

(6) *Most importantly, make prayer a natural and essential part of everyday living.* This is the point! The more natural a part of our lives is prayer and the presence of God, the more this will be reflected in our children as they grow and eventually have their own families. If Christianity is nothing but a contrived, tacked on part of life, we run the risk of it being nothing in the lives of our children as they mature. Then, we can cry out all we want and say, "We didn't raise them that way. We raised them to be

The Family That Prays and Plays Together

Christians." But it won't help much. It will be too late and, tragically, many will not even know what they did wrong. *They thought the "form" of Christianity was real Christianity, when it wasn't real at all* (Matt. 7:21-23).[17]

Why shouldn't the Christian family "enjoy" prayer and use every aspect of family recreation to the honor and glory of Christ? Why shouldn't every aspect of our family lives be seen as an important part of our commitment to God? When this is the case, then we are raising our children in the way of God. Even in our prayer, God must be supreme! *In the end, the real point of Christianity — what Christianity is all about — is not evangelism (as important as that is), but to strive to be at one with God. This is the essence of the Christian quest.* And, quite a quest it is! Prayer is essential to this quest. As Jane Austen (1775-1817) once said, "Grant us grace, Almighty Father, so to pray as to deserve to be heard." Remember: God DOES make house calls!

---

[17]This is the problem with fairly large groups within the Restoration Movement heritage, as well as with other groups characterized by legalism.

CHAPTER TEN

The Family Today

Interestingly, when we study the family in the Bible we get a rather different picture than the "nuclear family" we normally think of today.[1]

> The Old Testament family is a wider circle than the typical two-generation nuclear family of parents and children characteristic of contemporary Western society. It consists of those who share a common blood and common dwelling-place. It also includes servants, resident aliens (gerim) and stateless persons, widows and orphans, who live under the protection of the head of the family, as well as his wife (or wives and concubines if he is a polygamist) and children (see Gn. 7:1, 7; 46:8-26). Though from the first the divine intention was that marriage (see Sexuality*) should be monogamous (Gn. 2:21-24), . . ."[2]

The Hebrew term *mispahah* really has no exact equivalent in English, but can be interpreted as "household." "Another term for family, *bayith*, included all living within the confines and jurisdiction of the dwelling."[3]

In the New Testament as well, the word "household" is

---

[1] A helpful book is Dolores Curran, *Traits of a Healthy Family: Fifteen Traits Commonly Found in Healthy Families by Those Who Work with Them* (Minneapolis: Winston Press, 1983).

[2] *New Dictionary of Theology*, Edited by Sinclair B. Ferguson, David F. Wright, and J.I. Packer (Downers Grove, IL: InterVarsity Press, 1988), 251.

[3] *The New International Dictionary of the Bible*, General Editor, Merrill C. Tenney, Revising Editor J. D. Douglas (Grand Rapids: Zondervan, 1987), p. 343.

Serving Christ: A Family Affair

not simply a synonym for "family" as we think of it today. A "household" often consisted not only of father, mother, and children, but also of slaves, various dependents, such as servants, employees and even "clients" (e.g., freedmen or friends) who voluntarily joined themselves to a household for the sake of mutual benefits (Matt. 21:33ff.). Luke says that breaking of bread took place in the Jerusalem church "by households" (Acts 2:46). The household seems also to have had an important role in the establishment, growth and stability of the church.[4] "In the Jerusalem church households were apparently instructed as units (Acts 5:42), and this was also Paul's custom, as he reminded the Ephesian elders (Acts 20:20)." It seems that a "regular catechesis[5] existed setting forth the mutual duties of members of a Christian household: wives and husbands, children and fathers, servants and masters. See Col. 3:18-4:1; Eph. 5:22-6:9; 1 Pet. 2:18-3:7."[6]

The family unit is a basic part of the structure of creation. The family relationship is the institution of God lying at the foundation of all human society. "From the beginning it is God's purpose that mankind should increase by families, not as isolated individuals."[7] Parental

---

[4]The households of Cornelius (Acts 10:7, 24), Lydia and the Jailer (Acts 16:15, 31-34, Stephanas (1 Cor. 15:16), Crispus and Gaius (Acts 18:8; 1 Cor. 1:14-16; Rom. 16:23), Prisca and Aquila (at Ephesus, 1 Cor. 16:19; and perhaps Rome, Rom. 16:5), Oneisphorus (2 Tim. 1:16; 4:19), Philemon (Phil. 1-2), Nymphas or Nympha (Col. 4:15), Asyncritus and Philologus (Rom. 16:14-15) are mentioned by name in the New Testament.

[5]Instruction of one who is being taught the principles of Christianity. A "catechism" was a short book giving, in question-and-answer form, a brief summary of the basic principles of a religion.

[6]*New Bible Dictionary*, Edited by J.D. Douglas, F.F. Bruce, J.I. Packer, et. al., Second Edition (Wheaton, IL: Tyndale House Publishers, 1982), p. 372.

[7]Ibid.

obligations include the maintenance of children (1 Tim. 5:8) and their education in its fullest sense (Exod. 12:26-27; Deut. 6:6-7; Eph. 6:4). The family occupies a prominent place throughout the Bible. It is the first form of society. God intended it to be the bud (and representative) of every fellowship. Yet the family as we now know it is often without function and is no longer necessarily the basic unit in our society.

Thus, in both Testaments the family is much broader, and much more important, than we normally see it being in our day. With regard to the family one thing is absolutely clear in the Bible. Nowhere in Scripture is there found the idea that each "family" consists of two parents and 2.3 children living in a house on a lot 100 by 60 feet and as an isolated unit, with a "King and Queen" and a three-bedroom home as their little "castle." *In the Bible, the family was too broad and too important for such isolation.* But with the modern view of the nuclear family, it is no wonder that that institution and the church are in serious trouble today. Dr. Paul Popenoe of the American Institute of Family Relations uttered an ominous note: 'No society has ever survived after its family life deteriorated.'"[8]

The "Nuclear" Family Today

Actually, the concept of the "nuclear" family of today — "the typical two-generation nuclear family of parents and children characteristic of contemporary Western society" — is not only foreign to the Bible; it is relatively new in the history of America as well. We have been doing some personal family history recently. As a result, we have found that in the 1920s, for example, over 50 percent of the families in America included at least one extra adult. Up until that time, families that immigrated

---

[8]Gangel, *The Family First*, p. 127.

Serving Christ: A Family Affair

from Europe were almost always extended families. Even now, immigrant families, no matter where they come from, are often extended families; e.g., grandparents, aunts, uncles, cousins, etc. We would argue that this is one aspect that contributes often to making immigrant families so vital.

There certainly does seem to be confusion today as to what a family is. The word "family" has been stretched and pulled out of context until it has ceased to mean anything at all to some people. But what worries us more is that so often it seems "family" has ceased to mean anything at all to people who should know what it means — and that so many of these "families" are found in churches today. While it is true that "family" was broader than sometimes viewed today, it is also true that essentially, the *family* is based on the union of a man and a woman and the children they beget. But as we have seen, "family" need not be limited to just parents and biological offspring — especially in the Christian sense.

Whatever else some may tell you, it is also true that God created man and woman and gave them the ability to reflect their union in the most beautiful way possible — by together bringing forth a baby, a new being who is part of each of them. *It takes imagination, commitment, hard work, love, grace, patience, and time to become what God intended a family to be*! If we could only get the truth, solidly implanted in our very beings, that it takes *unconditional commitment* and the *most serious effort* to truly become a family and to maintain and mature *as a family* half the battle would be won.

But given this "definition" of family, we are not interested in "arguing" about what does or doesn't constitute a "family" or who is or isn't a family, because this will not help the real issue at hand. Nor are we interested in telling people that they are or aren't a "family." Certainly, it is clear that there are other forms of "family" besides

The Family Today

the "nuclear family." The Scripture talks about the family of God (2 Cor. 6:18; Gal. 3:26; Eph. 2:19) and of families "in heaven and on earth" (Eph. 3:15). We are interested in helping people work through whatever kind of "unit" they have — if possible — to become closer to the Lord and to build a Christian family that will minister![9]

Yet it is important to talk about the family as it is exists today. The division of families into age-level groups with their own social activities and childcare left to those outside the family has not been good for the American family.[10] The whole structure of American families has changed. Education has become the job of schools — public or private. Religion has become the task of the church. Even athletic experiences are "jobbed out" to others such as the Little League, etc. It seems, parents are no longer responsible for anything in the lives of their children.

We are not going to argue here which came first, "the chicken or the egg." Some could say that the need for childcare outside the home came first from the need to have two incomes in order to survive economically. We might well argue that the real "need" for childcare outside the home often comes from the "success ethic" of American culture. Surely, no one will argue that the decline of moral values, the divorce rate, and the relegation of children to care outside the home has helped the

---

[9] Perhaps it is important to say here that, following scriptural mandates, we condemn the sin, but *not the sinner*; e.g., we can see no way scripturally that a homosexual union can ever be considered a "Christian" family.

[10] But I [Terry] want to be very clear that we *know* mothers who work outside the home can be good mothers. We have known many, many wonderful mothers who worked outside the home, either because they had to, or because they chose to pursue a career. The real issue is the love of the mother and the quality of the time spent with the child. The mere fact that a mother is in the home 24 hours a day doesn't automatically make her a "good mother" either.

Serving Christ: A Family Affair

American family? As we have said, more than six million of America's children now live in homes divided by divorce.[11] Most of these children will suffer effects well into adulthood — and so will our society for decades to come!

The essential assignment for the Christian family is to relate assertively and positively to the realities of today's world without being caught up in, or controlled by, secular society's powerful influences. This will only happen when the Christian family sees itself as an inseparable and ministering unit engaging society at every point of contact. We must first be sure that "family" really means something again, then understand "what" it means, and, finally, implement this in society. This will not happen without commitment and values, God as the bedrock of the family.

Today's "Success Ethic"

The "success ethic" of 20th century America stands clearly and forcefully in opposition to the Christian ethic and is having devastating consequences for the family. What is the "success ethic"? Simply put, the only "ethic" is success! Basically, it is the approach that all that counts is money, power, and position. We live in a society where might not only "makes right," but where authority, or power, is often seen as equivalent to righteousness. This is true in all too many homes, businesses, governments, churches, and TV ministries.

Get ahead at any cost! After all, we have to provide "things" for our children, don't we? In the name of providing for the American family, almost any kind of neglect is justified. Our society's economic foundation rests on consumption. We so clearly teach our children to

---

[11]CBS Evening News, 5 March 1995.

The Family Today

buy, buy, buy, eat, eat, eat, and to always be on the go or — somehow, the message is — we will fall apart as a society. When, in fact, this exact behavior is precisely what is causing us to fall apart! As Wesley said, "Let no man deceive you with vain words; riches and happiness seldom dwell together. Therefore, if you are wise, you will not seek riches for your children. . . . Aim simply at the glory of God, and the real happiness of your children, both in time and eternity."[12]

This success "ethic" is steadily eroding society! Tragically, it is not just "secular" society that is materialistic and measures one's worth by one's properties — just look at many of the new "mega-churches" if you want to see Materialism baptized in the name of church growth. Again, as Augustine saw so clearly, as sinful persons we are self-centered beings, prone to choose self over God. This centering on self leads even more to being enticed by worldly things even in a Christian family. Oh, it has some very subtle "elements." It is an ethic in which we decide what is "right" by asking what works. It is an ethic where masses of Christians have become insensitive to injustice — especially that which springs from privilege, power, class, sex, race, and position. Are there any other kinds?

Unfortunately, many Christians do not see this even though they are a real part of it! We are judged as successful by what we *do* not by who we *are*. We are judged to be successes by how much *money* we make, *power* we have, by what *others* think of us. What is even worse, we are clearly teaching this "ethic" to our children! They see all too precisely just what and who are really important to us. What they see is a materialistic world that measures one's worth by one's assets, not by one's attributes and

---

[12]John Wesley, *Sermons*, "On Family Religion," (1788), III, p. 17; in Jackson, *The Works of the Rev. John Wesley, A.M.*, Vol. VII, p. 85.

Serving Christ: A Family Affair

commitments. We, undoubtedly, live in one of the most materialistic societies in the history of the world. The paired evils at the black heart of materialism are *competitive greed* and *self-centered individualism*.

This problem is so pronounced that a recent TV commercial illustrates the situation, while poking fun at it. Pictured before us is a large beautifully wood-paneled boardroom. It is in the evening and business as usual is still being conducted. Without warning one man looks at his watch, closes his folder of notes, gets up from his chair and walks toward the door. Everyone at the table is stunned. You can see the tension as if they think he — or they — will be struck down because of his action. Reaching the door, the man looks back, says, "'Pinocchio' is on at eight o'clock," and leaves. Then, we hear a voice say, "Parents who have the Disney channel have different priorities." If only this were always true.

"Success" for the Christian couldn't be any more removed from the mindset in that boardroom. For Jesus "successful" is synonymous with being "faithful," to Him and our fellows; by *being* a certain way, not by *doing* anything as such! For the Christian there are many values infinitely more important than how "much" of anything we have. Now to be sure, *being* something means we will strive to act with integrity, i.e., with love, joy, peace — Galatians 5:22-23 — etc., but the "being" is the *essential* basis for the "doing." Yes, even "activism" in the name of God is less than effective if the "doing" is not based on the "being." We have known many a Christian who "worked themselves to death" for their cause, when it was clear they, not to mention their families, would have been much better off if they had spent more time at home.

Many TV "ministries" aren't much more than money raising machines. Many have been exposed for what they were. Christians should be very careful before they support anything they see on TV.[13] We know the "ministry" of a prominent television "evangelist" very well. Almost the first day of our exposure, one of the chief lieutenants told Terry that what really mattered — the unquestionable bottom line — to this prominent evangelist was "nickels and numbers." The whole ministry was *pervaded* by the "bigger is greater" success syndrome! Thank the Lord that many are seeing through this subtle evil. The "doing," e.g., bigger numbers, more money, more more more *never* make us successes, any more than does the perceived lack of it in the eyes of others make us *failures*. It is the "being" that makes us a success!

"Values" and Today's Family

You didn't have to pick up this book to know the family is in trouble. We have more than alluded to this fact and to some of the reasons it is true. And, yet, trouble in American families is not brand new. The family has been "written off" long ago. Like the town crier in colonial times in Britain and America, modern social scientists (and some other scholars) have been announcing the death of the American family for more than a generation now. *The institution of the family will not die!* Of this, we can be absolutely sure. God will not let this happen. But the extent to which it is seriously ill may be partially attributable to these "nay-sayers" self-fulfilling prophecies!

These "death chants" have been rather amazing when you think about it. Certainly, we find there a realization that the family as an institution is in serious trouble, but

---

[13]We recommend that Christians channel all their giving through their local congregation, and that they check out very, very carefully any ministry not supported by their local congregation before supporting it. The use — abuse — of religion (and of starving children) has always been one of best ways to accumulate ill-gotten fortunes.

Serving Christ: A Family Affair

the obituaries are premature! The patient *is* ill, but has not died yet! These "scientists" and "scholars" have laughed at the family as a possible force for values development and the recovery of society for over twenty years now. But there has been no suggestion of a viable alternative institution to replace the family as the very core of society. Here we are two decades later and still no real candidate has emerged to take over the historical role of family in society. There is none, there will be none — the family, in God, is our only hope!

Yet with all this gloomy view of the family and its future, in 1975 the United States Senate was saying that "families are the most vital and fundamental institutions of this nation and the families are experiencing numerous difficulties and pressures in an increasingly complex, technological society."[14] Although we hear the phrase "family values" used today by all kinds of questionable sources, much of the problem with today's families *does* have to do with "values." But it is one thing to "promote" values because of a political agenda, or "preach" values because of an institutional (church) agenda; and quite another to understand what they are, how fundamental they are to, and how to implement them in, the Christian family.

We have known many rather "typical" families — and on the face of it "good" families — during our ministries. One example from Southern California comes to mind. The father was an administrator in the public schools and a deacon. The mother was a church secretary. They lived comfortably in an upper middle class neighborhood. Both were very active in the church and in the drama group we helped start there. Neither of their two children

---

[14]In a bill entitled "Family and Household Research Act of 1975" which referred to a Senate Subcommittee on Children and Youth statement. The purpose of the bill was simply to broaden the knowledge of the pressures on families.

chose the parents' Christianity. The son was arrested for selling drugs out of the home, ended up getting a young girl pregnant, and dying *very* young. The daughter was so wild at 13 no one could control her. From middle grade school, when the family came to church, the children were allowed to stay and play in the car! The story could go on and on. But the parents saw themselves as dedicated Christians. Being a Vice Principal in charge of discipline, the father was the first one to jump on the "bandwagon" with regard to the need for discipline. Yet his own family had none.

Researchers will tell you that families with problems like the one mentioned above are not uncommon in our changing society. In fact, today it seems like they are in the majority. Maybe *Roseanne* (mentioned in the "Introduction") is more representative than we dare admit. Most unfortunately, such folks are not uncommon among church families either. They are very often the result of confused values. As numerous cultural pressures bear down on the child, he or she must make early choices about values. Without considerable *real* support in the home, a child's values will naturally reflect the dominate influences on him or her. When will we learn this powerful truth!

The truth of the matter is that if our children are not clear about their values at a fairly early age as modeled in the home, as the natural desire for independence comes with adolescence it may well be too late! *You are responsible for what you let your children do and who they associate with*. If they have really been on the verge of being "out of control" as young children, then why be surprised when they *are* out of control as teens?

On the other hand, don't despair too soon. In even the best of homes adolescents will test the boundaries. If you have done your "work" well up to this point, you can afford to let them range a little. Sometimes this "testing"

Serving Christ: A Family Affair

will take what seems to you interesting, if not "bizarre," forms. We knew of the child of one member of the Congress of the United States. The son became very conservative in his political thinking, obviously challenging part of his home life.

It is somewhat "natural" for children to range afield in the opposite direction of the parents. Sometimes this "ranging" is a "needed midcourse correction." With love, patience, guidance, and a firm hand when needed, these midcourse corrections can often have positive results. Whatever you do, DON'T PANIC! When you do, you either make things worse, or give the child the idea that the situation is hopeless. And, you will find, sometimes deep under the surface, that even "wayward" children need and want hope! You may need to seek outside help, but be very careful to get the best help possible.

We must be clear about Christian values and assert these above secular values. We must model these to the church and to society. *Surely, many Christian values should be abundantly clear; for example, the sanctity of marriage and commitment to it; developing the home as a place of warmth, nurture, acceptance, and healthy stimulation; learning of God through His Word; growing in grace together and as individuals; implementing the teaching of Scripture by modeling a just, merciful, and loving lifestyle; and involvement in outreach through the church and as a family participating in God's redeeming work in society.*

The Lack of Communication

At the heart of many of the problems with today's families is not only a serious lack of communication, but seemingly, an almost total lack of understanding as to what communication is and why it is so vital to families. We mentioned communication as one of the "keys" to a successful marriage in the "Preface" and we talk about it throughout the book. Consequently, you will not be surprised to learn that much research (over the last 30 years) in how values are developed exposes a close relationship between communication styles the child experiences and the development of higher structures of values. In the King James Version, 1 Corinthians 15:33 reads, "Evil communications corrupt good manners."[15] Whether this translation is best or not, there is certainly something to that thought.

We so take "communication" for granted! We talk of "communication gaps" or "generation gaps" (which *are* communication gaps), but do not understand the cause is *defective* communication. In the church, for some unknown reason we think "preaching," the perfect example of one way "communication," works, even though the word itself is used in everyday speech in a pejorative manner. We need to "get out of the box"! In our family relationships we talk "at" each other rather than "with" each other. But people were meant to "communicate" in deep and wonderful ways. Why else would we have been created in God's image?

Terry has a story he "claims" is true. He has often said that he thinks about how much he loves me during the day when I am at school, or even when standing by my side doing the dishes together [before we let the dishwasher take over]. He claims he had these thoughts for years, before he realized that just because he thought about how much he loved me, even if I was standing right beside him, if he didn't verbalize it I would never know! Mere "thought" doesn't convey the message. Who among us doesn't need to *hear* the words, doesn't need personal reassurance, once in a while? In fact, we both readily admit, the more we "reassure" each other, the

---

[15]Better translated, "Do not be deceived: 'Bad company corrupts good morals.'" This is important for parents to remember!

Serving Christ: A Family Affair

happier we are![16] Sharing — meaningful communication — *is* "key" to a marriage. It has to be worked at, and worked at daily! It simply cannot and must not be taken for granted.

We must learn to truly listen to one another, to want to hear what is actually being said, and to convince our "significant other" that we do really want to understand. We must encourage the other person to help us understand their point of view. We must develop loving and lively communication styles with our mates and our children so that we will not only hear and understand them; but so they will see that we really do care not only about what they are saying, and why, but also really care about them — how they are actually feeling inside.

"Nontraditional" Families

In thinking about the family in today's world, one is forced to recognize both the complexity of the issue and that we can no longer afford to make certain assumptions. As we have said, not all families are "nuclear families," nor have they ever been. Sociologists talk about "Alternative Styles of Marriage" (ASM). There were many ASM's in early 19th century America; for example, there were numerous communal experiments with variations in family forms like the Shakers (who espoused celibacy), and the New Harmony (Indiana) colony of Robert Owen.[17]

Further back hundreds of years in church history, we see in the Roman Catholic tradition (and others as well)

---

[16]Here is another very important "tip" to a successful marriage! Reassure each other often!

[17]Owen (1771-1858) was a British industrialist and social reformer who believed that man's character is formed by his environment. In New Harmony, he experimented with education, science, and communal living as a means to create a model Community of Equality. The experiment in Indiana lasted only from 1825-1827. Owen had been

monks, priests, and nuns living in community. Thus, there is a long history of belief that aspects of the faith demanded other than "Traditional Family Forms (TFF)." The Apostle Paul certainly made a case for celibacy, and for marriage (albeit, on the surface at least a rather negative one, 1 Corinthians 7:1-9, 32-35.). According to sociologists, "there are at least ten different ASM which in one way or another modify TFF." They are: trial marriage, ad hoc arrangements, singleness, single parenthood, child-free marriage, communal living, group marriage, mate swapping, gay marriage, and dual-career marriage.[18] Obviously some of these are acceptable for Christians and have a long history, and some are not.

In a scant 20 years our ideas have changed (in some cases quite dramatically) — sometimes for the good and sometimes not — so that "dual-career marriage" would hardly be considered "Alternative Styles of Marriage" today. Writing in 1975, Christian sociologist John Scanzoni makes an interesting comment:

> The notion that work or vocation is a sacred calling from God permeates the whole Bible, and nowhere, it seems to me, can defensible grounds be found to deny any vocations to married women. . . . It therefore follows that women should be free to pursue their vocations as diligently as do men, in other

---

influenced by the utilitarian thought of his business partner, Jeremy Bentham. Owen was a universalist, and perceived by many as an atheist. He debated publicly with Alexander Campbell on the merits of organized religion in Cincinnati in 1829. The debate was published by Campbell as *Debate on the Evidences of Christianity*.

[18]For a brief discussion of these see John Scanzoni, "A Christian Perspective on Alternative Styles of Marriage," in Gary R. Collins, Editor, *Make More of Your Marriage* (Waco, TX: Word Books, 1976), pp. 157-168. See also Letha & John Scanzoni, *Men, Women, and Change: A Sociology of Marriage and Family* (New York: McGraw-Hill, 1976).

words to seek to achieve to the fullest extent of their God-given gifts. The best biblical model of this "emerging" ASM is Priscilla and Aquila.

We agree that Priscilla and Aquila are an interesting model and that "prevailing forms (TFF) are [sometimes] unsatisfactory for many reasons, . . . they permit men to be selfish (often unconsciously), women to be exploited (often by default), and the church and society to be deprived of the gifts God has given to women." We think it is important that

> . . . Christians . . . respond positively to the difficulties and opportunities [ASM] brings. To do otherwise will mean we have learned nothing from the mistakes of our fathers in other areas (for example, political, racial, economic discrimination) and to misread both "the signs of the times" and the Scriptures.[19]

It is important to recall that, as Locke said, "New opinions are always suspected, and usually opposed, without any other reason but because they are not already common."[20] However, we don't think any ASM should be accepted uncritically. We certainly agree with Scanzoni's comment regarding work.[21]

Today, that percentage — of over 50 percent of the families which included at least one extra adult

---

[19]John Scanzoni, "A Christian Perspective on Alternative Styles of Marriage," p. 166.

[20]Locke, *Essay Concerning Human Understanding*, "Dedicatory Epistle."

[21]See Miethe, "God and the Day's Work" in *The New Christian's Guide to Following Jesus*, pp. 117-122; and Robert Lowry Calhoun, *God and the Day's Work: Christian Vocation in an Unchristian World* (New York: Fleming H. Revell Company, 1943); W.R. Forrester, *Christian Vocation: Studies in Faith and Work* (New York: Charles Scribner's Sons, 1953); Francis O. Ayres, *The Ministry of the Laity: A Biblical Exposition* (Philadelphia: Westminster Press, 1962); Elton Trueblood, *The Company of the Committed* (New York: Harper & Row, 1961); Larry

The Family Today

(mentioned in the last chapter) — has dropped to less than 5 percent as we relegate grandparents, aunts, uncles, and others to a lonely existence in retirement homes, nursing homes, and worse — to the streets. Nowadays we not only have the phenomenon of "unwanted" family members; we have the disintegration of the family on all sides. Wherever you get the statistic, there is an incredible percentage of one parent families, children with no parents, and homeless people roaming the streets of America. These are all people who were also created in God's image, who deserve to be ministered to and to have the opportunity to minister.

Nowadays, many are experiencing a growing "new" phenomenon — grown and/or married offspring coming "back to the nest" as has been spoofed on TV in *The Boys Are Back*. We have heard much joking about looking forward to the "empty nest" only to find it occupied again. Usually, when a grown child comes back to live at home it is because of a financial or other crisis. While each individual household needs to deal with such an occurrence according to their ability, we think (as long as the child or children are not trying to take unfair advantage) it is quite consistent with the biblical model of the extended household to help our grown children if we can!

Certainly, *we* would want to help our son and his family. In such a case, it is important, as parents, to do everything in our power not to impact negatively our offspring's dignity or "adulthood." We must give them "space" and treat them as equals, as adults. At the same time, it will be best if a clear "understanding" is mutually agreed upon with regard to the offspring's responsibilities in the home. It is not inappropriate to expect them to

---

Peabody, *Secular Work is Full-Time Service* (Fort Washington, PA: Christian Literature Crusade, 1974); Leland Ryken, *Work & Leisure in Christian Perspective* (Portland, OR: Multnomah Press, 1987).

Serving Christ: A Family Affair

contribute to the well-being of the home ("spiritually" or otherwise), to share duties around the house, or to contribute financially toward food and expenses as agreed upon — and as they are able.

Individuals need help to develop an understanding of and skills in fulfilling ministry as God ordained it. In the New Testament, the widows ministered to young wives. These older women were not to be "malicious gossips, nor enslaved to much wine, teaching what is good" (Titus 2:3); so they may teach the young women "how to love their husbands and children" (vs. 4, RSV). Every family member has a duty to help others in need. This ministry should go on in "traditional" families as the members of these families minister to nontraditional families. In many nontraditional families, we need to help in developing "lifestyle changes." Lifestyle changes require, among other things, socialization; i.e., "sharing a total way of living that encompasses beliefs, values, attitudes, emotions, and behavior." These must be both taught and modeled. "This kind of life-style development is clearly implied in both the Old and New Testament."[22]

The "bottom line" is that while the church must not forget that it is an extension of the family, the church and "traditional" families must not forget they have a responsibility to include, share with, and minister to those persons in society who may not be a part of traditional families. The church, in any age, will always be judged by how it treats the sick, the downtrodden, the hungry, the homeless — the needy — of society! Here, again, we MUST get out of the box and think of caring and creative ways to address the needs of the needy. May it never be that, as Christians, we become callous to helping those *who are truly in need*!

---

[22] Larry Richards, "How the Church Can Help the Family Face the Future" in Collins' *Facing the Future,* p. 13.

The Family Today

One final word, by way of example. Terry has often said that the church today may well be judged — by man and by God — as to whether it is truly Christ's church by how we respond to the AIDS crisis. We know that this is a "touchy" and "unpleasant" subject for many, but the need to respond is growing every day, even in small towns in the Midwest where more and more AIDS sufferers are coming home to die. Let us be clear, *we* do not accept drug use or homosexuality as biblically valid "alternative lifestyles." We would not personally support any organization that views AIDS as an extension of a philosophy that these unbiblical lifestyles are acceptable. However, once a person has contracted the disease — however they got it, whether through homosexuality or drug use, or whatever — they are still people for whom Christ died and deserve to be loved, ministered to, and treated with respect — and helped to "die" (if that be the only option) with dignity![23]

We must give thought to "nontraditional" families, how they can be ministered to and how we can include them in ministry.[24] The church must reach out to nontraditional families, as should "traditional" ones. The "Nuclear" family *must* reach out to nontraditional ones if the Body of Christ is to be what it should be! (John 13:34-35) Programs which "adopt" singles, grandparents, or another family member can offer hours of valuable experiences.

---

[23]See Wendell Hoffman & Stanley Grenz, *AIDS: Ministry in the Midst of an Epidemic*, 1990; Earl E. Shelp & Ronald H. Sunderland, *AIDS and the Church: The Second Decade*, Revised and enlarged (Philadelphia: Westminster/John Knox Press, 1987), 238 pages; and also by Shelp & Sunderland, *AIDS: A Manual for Pastoral Care*.

[24]The following may have some helpful ideas: Robert G. Barnes, Jr. *Single Parenting: A Wilderness Journey* (Wheaton, IL: Tyndale House Publishers, 1984. Andre & Fay Bustanoby, *The Readymade Family* (Grand Rapids: Zondervan, 1982). Emily B. & John S. Visher, *Stepfamilies: A Guide to Working with Stepparents and Stepchildren* (New York: Brunner/Mazel Publishers, 1983).

Always, We Must Hope

One aspect of this whole "mess" of the modern American "family" is the not-so-subtle undercutting of the marriage relationship. As a student of history, recently teaching a college course on ancient Greek and Roman history, Terry doubts there has ever been a society more constantly bombarded by sex and lewd behavior. It is everywhere we turn. We are saturated with sex — in advertising, on daytime as well as nighttime TV, in the way we dress, think, and act. It is so easy to become caught up in this! Why can't we see what it is doing to society? But what bothers us the most is the larger effect. All this conditions us to accept the argument that the competitive and spiteful behavior we see all around is "normal" marriage, when in fact such behavior leads to broken marriages!

As we have seen time and again, parents can share, in the positive sense, only what is *real* about *their* relationship with God with their children. A family who doesn't have God as real in their lives cannot share ministry with those in need. As families, we are "to love the Lord your God and to serve Him with all your heart and all your soul" (Deut. 11:13) so that we may receive the rewards of obedience. This sharing must be a part of the flow of everyday life and experience. This is the most "natural way" to minister to others in need. Also, we must stop making people who choose celibacy, or who are unable to have children, feel like "second class citizens" in God's family![25]

---

[25]See Vicky Love, *Childless Is Not Less* (Minneapolis: Bethany House, 1984).

CHAPTER ELEVEN
The Family and Ministry

The very best way for a Christian family to minister is to do what families do naturally, as families, and include others in the circle. Actually, we have already said much about "family ministry." For, you see, when a "Christian family" is *being* a Christian family, when its members are maturing and being nurtured in the Lord (when it is engaging in all of the aspects that make it Christian), it is ministering. We really do not want to perpetuate the "sacred" versus "secular" dichotomy! Activities should not be so quickly divided into categories of "religious" and "non." Most anything that a Christian family should be doing, or can do profitably, can, with a little creative forethought, be used to minister. Bear in mind, our goal as Christians is not necessarily to "preach" at everyone who comes within earshot. In our experience, such "preaching" is ultimately counterproductive — not to mention hypocritical.

The individual family, too, needs quiet and private time. The separate members of the family can still be ignored when the family as a whole is "constantly" out serving others. Even "ministry" should not divide or separate the family. *Family time is, in the end, sacred — because the family is a divine institution.* It isn't just how many hours, but the quality of time we spend as a family, and as a family in ministry, that counts. Another former professor of Terry's had a sign in his office window, "It's not how many hours a day you're awake that counts, it's

Serving Christ: A Family Affair

what you do when you are that matters." "Workaholism" is NOT Christian, and it sure can be used by Satan.

We also agree with one of our professors who taught us that the time used in preparation for ministry *is* ministry. This is important to keep in mind especially in a world that seems to prize "activism" — the mere doing of something, anything — rather than using the mind or study. What we are saying here is that it is not an either/or; i.e., studying or serving. Real, serious, yes, even *effective* ministry takes real, serious, effective preparation! Look, for example, at the biblical models of Moses, John the Baptist, Jesus, and Paul. Each prepared many, many years for a much shorter period of what most would call "actual service."[1]

Yet the primary purpose of this chapter is to give some suggestions about how a family can minister together, remembering that ministry is also preparation and is not activism.

(1) Spend time together reading God's Word and discussing its moral meaning. Surely, this is time well spent which will give rewards in turn to every aspect of life, to everything we do in life. Again, "preparation" is ministry. We cannot emphasize too strongly that the family needs to "prepare" for effective ministry. This means praying and teaching in the home, as well as taking advantage of the programs of the church to prepare the family to minister. And, why not occasionally include someone outside the family in this reading and/or study. Remember, the "trick" is for the Christian family to model every aspect of what it is to be a "Christian family" to others and to include others in its activities. What could be more effective ministry?

---

[1] Important discussions of this are found in Miethe, *The New Christian's Guide to Following Jesus*, in "Ministry and the Christian," pp. 103-110 and in "God and the Day's Work," pp. 117-122.

The Family and Ministry

(2) Discuss moral and ethical issues and arrive at judgments together as a family before individual members have to be confronted by tempting situations. One of the real problems when we are confronted with a "moral dilemma" is that we are so often unprepared for the test or temptation. Surely, the best way to handle such times is to be prepared by having discussed the situations and what the options are for a Christian response. Doesn't this seem like it would be helpful, not to mention prudent, for the adults and children in the family to discuss ethical issues and dilemmas they may have to confront and be as thoroughly prepared as possible. Why is it that policemen, firemen, and military personnel "train" beforehand how to handle a situation? Surely, because this is the best way to minimize fear and inappropriate responses. This will not "guarantee" that the "right" action will be taken, but it will sure help.

(3) Help all concerned to see marriage and the family in the best possible light. This is another of the aspects of family life we must not take for granted. It takes work to make a marriage and a family strong. Some special time should be regularly set aside for the spouse and for individual members of the family, besides for the family as a whole. Being fairly new in their lives together, John and Nicole take one night a week to be alone together. Very important and wise. (Not to mention that Grandpa and Granny get to see Britain at least one night a week for sure!) But having some special time together is just as important, if not more so, as the years race by. To take your spouse, marriage, or family for granted will eventually bring a slow and certain death to a marriage. If you have a large family, perhaps one special evening a month for each child would be possible, or a few hours on a certain day. The issue here is to make everyone in the family know that they are important as individuals. Again, this will overflow into all aspects of life and witness.

Serving Christ: A Family Affair

(4) Programs to "adopt" singles, grandparents, and others as family members can be effective and meaningful with regard to family ministry. Again, the "trick" is to involve others in, and share the blessings of, the Christian family. There is no more effective way to minister. Such ministries are often most effective when the whole church organizes and administers the program because the church should be more familiar with the broader needs of the community and be able to effectively match up individuals with families that have "special" talents, experience, or training to meet individual needs. For example, a Christian family with a learning disabled child, or a handicapped child, may be able to give special comfort or help to a single parent in a similar situation. With families so scattered these days, that perhaps lonely "adopted" aunt, uncle, grandma, or grandpa might both minister to your children and be ministered to by your family. Shared ministry is the best of all possible worlds.

(5) Children love to play games. Family activities can include table games, puzzles, quizzes, ping pong, etc. Alma Jones in "Fun with Children" says, "Scientific studies show that maladjustments of children decrease as family recreation increases; also that understanding and confidence between parents and children increase as shared activities and good times increase."[2] Does it really take "scientific studies" to tell us that? It should be as obvious as the proverbial "nose on your face." Involve others in your game playing — another natural and easy way to witness.

You say, "But we may not say a whole lot about our faith when we play games." O.K., so what? But don't kid yourself. You will be modeling attitudes and relationships

---

[2] The American Institute of Family Relations, Publication No. 226.

and setting the stage so trust can develop, that when the time comes, the person will turn to you for help and advice about "spiritual" matters. Years ago, while Terry was driving Antony Flew around, Tony said, "If I can't believe a man when he talks to me about earthly things, why should I believe him when he talks to me about heavenly things?" Terry has never forgotten this. Flew got it exactly right! Personal integrity is really the "key." They will not turn to us for "spiritual" advice (or help), if they see that as individuals, or in our family relationships, we don't have integrity.

(6) Hobbies can be central to a family and very effectively used to minister. Hobbies such as camping; photography; interest in local or regional history; collecting, e.g., coins, stamps, shells, or anything else; can be interesting and educational. It is also possible to build small groups of families around such hobbies for an evening or two a month, Saturday or Sunday afternoon time, or on an outing together, and to use these groups for witnessing and even for evangelism. Think how much children can learn about the history, culture, and *religion* of a place — or the world — through many of these hobbies and how that can be related to Christianity! Initiative, insight, and creativity are important here.

(7) Unfortunately, TV is already the biggest user of family time, but properly used it can enhance education and preparation for and ministry itself. There are programs on many channels and networks which are good educational shows for the family to watch. Some even teach good moral lessons. Properly supervised, even many regularly scheduled shows can be used as "objective lessons" with regard to what not to do as well as what to do. As always, the parents must take the responsibility to view the show with this teaching, not to mention critical thinking, in mind.

Today, almost everyone has a VCR which can be used

Serving Christ: A Family Affair

to view specific material, some overtly Christian, that can be obtained from the public library, many church libraries, video rental stores, which can be used by the family to show to other families or children to teach. The members of the family could view the movie or show beforehand and "take notes" on important scenes which relate Christian values, morals, etc., so these could be discussed intelligently before and after the showing, so the content can be reviewed with the family and other families or children.

(8) Take along a friend whenever possible. We always encouraged our son to take along a friend if he so desired (if he didn't want to, that was fine too). Family outing and vacations are important. Even if we could afford to, we didn't fly to "X" city and then stay in the most expensive hotel.[3] For us, half the fun was getting there, exploring on the way and exploring after we arrived. On family outings we almost always took one of John's friends along. He enjoyed the company and the friend enjoyed the trip, as well. This continued up through college. In fact, we — grandpa, granny,[4] son, daughter, and grandson have just completed another joint family vacation on which we drove well over 3000 miles. We have already taken several together since John and Nicole have been married.

Be careful *not* to change your Christian habits to less "showy" ones — or vice versa — because non-family members are present. Bear in mind one of the most effective ministries a Christian family can *have* is to model what a Christian family *is* to others. We have had several

---

[3]To this day, John will tell you we always stayed in the cheapest place we could find. And, he would probably be right. After all, about the only time we spent in the motel room was to sleep and we don't do a lot of that on a family outing.

[4]Beverly's preferred title.

The Family and Ministry

children — even minister's children — over the years tell us that they wished they were part of our family. John has had school friends, or Scouting friends, want to go to church with us, simply because they felt it was so good to be a part of our family, and our family went to church, so maybe they should too! You don't have to preach. Frequently, it is amazing what a little *reality* will do in witness. If you have a larger family, then you may need to take the friend of one child at a time.

In regard to the outdoors, the possibilities are almost endless. There is camping, hiking, just walking, kite flying, sledding, ice skating, touch football, catch, tag, basketball, badminton, croquet, lawn darts, and on and on. Something as simple and as old as pitching horse shoes (rather than "pitching" a fit) can be great fun and be a chance for all kinds of meaningful communication. Remember: it isn't so much the activity as it is the attitude. The yard or outdoors can become just about anything you can dream it to be. Short trips for picnics to a nearby park, a bicycle ride, or a weekend camping trip can be incredibly rewarding, and can be used to model a lifestyle and provide very meaningful ministry. A "vacation" doesn't have to be long, far away, or expensive to be a happy and positive family experience or a productive time for ministry.

One of the things we need to do is to "slow down" our lives and get back to some of the more basic, simple, and tried and true fun activities of the past. These yard or outdoor activities can provide the most amazing teaching opportunities. You can naturally teach Christian character, attitudes, good sportsmanship, etc., while teaching them how to build a fire and survive outdoors. Almost amazing when you think about it. How often have any of us wished for a good Christian coach? One year there were ten little boys in Claremont, California who wanted to have a Webelos Den. They couldn't find a parent to serve — much, much too busy. Finally Terry, who was a full-time associate minister in a large church, on the District Advisory Council for the local schoolboard, and working on his second doctorate, etc., said "O.K. I'll take a year out of my academic program to do it for the boys." It was one of the most enjoyable years of his life.

(9) Share your house as a place for ministry with others. There are so many ways the home can be used creatively for ministry; e.g., hosting Bible studies, fellowship meetings, or simply inviting someone over to share. In Virginia we had a large house with two acres of ground. We volunteered as "dorm parents" for one floor of a local college dormitory. In this capacity we would sponsor and chaperon parties for the students sometimes at local parks or actually in our home. We had over 80 students in our home at one time! But more important than big gatherings, the students on that dorm floor knew if they needed to get away from campus for a while, or just needed some privacy, they were welcome in our home.[5] When John was in high school, the church youth group used our home more than they did the church. Use your home for God!

(10) Parents should be active in the child's school. Perhaps this should go without saying, but parents should be as actively involved in the school life of the child as possible. Make time to go on field trips with the child, serve as a room mother or father, be active in PTA or PFA, be active in the school district, etc. This can not only be fun and rewarding, but can help the parent know better the influences and pressures the child is under, as well as give the parent the opportunity to model their values and lifestyle to others at all levels in the school

---

[5]You don't have to be an actual part of the college community to do this. You might go through your church to find area college students or through an area campus ministry.

district.

(11) The family, even the young children, should be involved in ministries that feed the hungry, give to the poor, help the homeless, give comfort to the sick, etc. Most churches or communities have food banks, places that collect good used clothing for use by the needy and in disasters, meal programs, etc. Beverly's mother has long been involved in helping to prepare and serve meals for the needy during holidays. She spends Thanksgiving and the Christmas season feeding hundreds of others. *We think it is important to get our young children involved in such activities as soon as possible.* They can learn much from helping firsthand. We have driven for Meals on Wheels. In our opinion, Habitat for Humanity is one of the best "parachurch" ministries going!

We are not at all against "social" ministry. We simply can't "dispense" our Christian responsibility just by standing on the steps of our nice church building, or on the street corner, preaching *at* people. Being involved in helping society at large is important and certainly sanctioned in the New Testament. And, while we participate in many of these, we feel that as much as possible, and as often as possible, the ministries we support should be actually attempting to share the gospel with the people to whom they are ministering. We know that this is not always an option at the time, but as much as possible we think there should be a "verbal" witness rather than just "giving" some "thing" away.

Involve the whole family in children's outreach ministries and street ministries. It is important for the family, as a family, to get out of itself once in a while and to see and experience the needs of others. If at all possible expose yourself and your children to inner-city ministries. There are *so many* needs out there. This will help them see the depths of the ministry needs, help them to be truly thankful for what they have, and help

Serving Christ: A Family Affair

make them sensitive to the needs in the world when they are adults. Hopefully, they will do more about them than we have!

(12) Husband and wife and children can be involved in ministry by helping to bring others, children and adults, to church. Pick someone up and being them to church in the family car, or participate in a van ministry, etc. For years, and at different times, we were an extension of the vehicle "fleet" of the church. If you are going that way in the first place, it is simply good stewardship to bring someone else when possible. We know a wonderful (and, naturally, somewhat eccentric) English woman, named Elizabeth. Retired and on a fixed income, she uses her little petrol efficient auto continually for the church. We have often praised her selflessness. The taxi companies make a great deal of money for the service she gives without cost because it is a ministry to her.

(13) Use the family to take the church out into the community in every possible way. The truth of the matter is that every time a family member ventures out of its little nest, out into the world, that member should be taking the church into the community. As a minister, Terry has often heard church members lament about the fact that, unfortunately, people bring the world into the church. Certainly, this is true. But, if we only think about it, the opposite should be even more true. Each time a Christian goes out into the world there should be a shining light of faith surrounding them. Each of us, each member of the family, needs to see ourselves as *ministers* in every way, everyday as we go about living — living for Christ!

(14) Families should invite families to church. It has been documented over and over again, that the most effective evangelism occurs when families (as a natural extension of the family) invite others to be a part of *their* family of God. The more the church you are a part of

places an emphasis on the family, and the more your individual family reaches out as a family, the more naturally this witness and/or evangelism can take place. In this you will be limited only by your prayer, your sincerity — or your integrity — and desire to love those who so desperately need to have the love of God shared with them, and your willingness to "get out of the box" of tradition or apathy.

(15) Do not forget the ministry of prayer! We talked some about the family and prayer in chapter 9. Prayer is a ministry every Christian can and should have. It is, at one and the same time, the most powerful weapon in our arsenal and the most neglected. We would suggest that if a family or a congregation is truly serious about becoming what it can and should be, the place to begin is with a serious study of the biblical doctrine of prayer. Start by dropping to your knees and praying as earnestly as you can — by unmasking yourself before God. After all, He knows your heart anyway, doesn't He! Your "masks" are only fooling you, not Him! Serious, real revival always starts with serious, real prayer!

We have spent much time in England over the last decade and have learned so much from our experience. It is amazing how much that tiny island — technically it is no longer an island after the Chunnel — has contributed to the history of the world with regard to Christianity, art, literature, science, and many other fields. Many churches in England have "kneeling benches" built right into the back of the pews or "kneeling cushions" on hooks on the pew backs. We have used them often and find that kneeling together in prayer is a powerful symbol and a rich experience. We wonder if it wouldn't help if, in America, we would get into the habit of kneeling together in prayer again? Perhaps, this is just what we need — to "prostrate" ourselves before the Lord once more.

Again, ministry should be as natural a part of life as

Serving Christ: A Family Affair

life itself. Yet as an individual family, we cannot do everything, nor should we try. We must not lose our effectiveness by trying to go a thousand different directions at once. We will need to limit our activities according to the needs of the family, our preparation, our experience, and/or our willingness to be involved in serious preparation so that we will be effective. It might also be wise to change your major emphases in ministry every few years for several reasons.

CHAPTER TWELVE

The Family, Christian Education, and the World

We live in a society in which the importance of the home has been greatly reduced. Like some enemy lurking unseen in the shadows, some seem determined to even destroy family life all together. Historians have long argued that the disintegration of the family unit was a major factor in the decline and fall of past societies. Our own society's decline in family values is distressingly similar to that decline in the Roman Empire. In the introduction to the chapter on "Relationships, Marriage, and the Family" in the textbook Terry often uses in his college ethics class, the authors write, "Closely related to the state of marriage in our society is the state of the family."[1] It really doesn't take a "great mind" to see that the health of marriage and of the family is important to the health of society!

A few years ago, when then Vice President Dan Quayle spoke out on the problem of the decline of "family values," there was an incredible outcry against him. But, recently (April 1994) on the evening news, even one of the major networks reported the dramatic increase in unwed mothers and single parent families in the last 30 years and went on to relate the drastic decline in "family values" to what is happening in our society today. Today, you can hardly open the newspaper, turn on television, or even go to church without hearing horrific stories of

---

[1]Paul T. Jersild and Dale A. Johnson, *Moral Issues & Christian Response*, Fifth edition (Harcourt Brace College Publishers, 1993), p. 61.

child abuse which seem to have reached epidemic proportions! It is pretty clear that our own society's decline is related to the steady increase in dysfunctional families.

Many factors could be named as having contributed to the decline in the importance of the home as a family unit: divorce, substitute parents and fatherless children, low moral standards, materialism, strained family relations, a lack of an understanding of commitment, even television, just to name a few. But perhaps the most important factor in the waning importance of the home is what some have called "sociological detraction." This is the idea that the social functions carried on traditionally by, and in, the home have now been shifted to larger social groups. Certainly all of us who have school-age children know the plight of running ourselves ragged transporting our children to and from this or that function or practice. The family has to fight for any "togetherness" time. It should not have to do so!

Often, even the church is far from guiltless. Some congregations tend to "church the people to death." We know congregations that have meetings or functions for one or more elements of the family most every night. Usually these separate the family rather than unite it. This needs to stop. Therefore, let us seek to learn how Christian education relates to the family and the home, and how these in turn can impact the world.

Christian Education is *Essential*

In undergraduate school, we both had the privilege of studying under professor Gary Bussmann.[2] One of the wonderful and extremely powerful insights he helped us

---

[2]Professor Gerhard H. Bussmann is a fine Christian gentleman and a professor in the area of Christian Education. He also officiated at our wedding.

The Family, Christian Education, and the World

to see was that Christian education is the hope of the world! In the Greek text of the New Testament the word for teaching is used twice as much as the word for preaching. Christian education must be the bridge over which biblical theology or biblical content is transmitted to the individual Christian. We are not talking here about methods of teaching, or methods of running audiovisual equipment. So often we confuse Christian education with methodology. The method can never replace the content, which in this case is biblical theology.

In the last few weeks, after attending rather "typical" Sunday School classes, we are again convinced that the obvious reason for the confusion on the part of the average church member about what the Bible really teaches *is the great lack of real education, real teaching in the church*! We *must* start seeing the church as a "mini" college or seminary where real education takes place. We *must* provide opportunities in our churches for serious disciplined study, deep emotional sharing, and active meaningful service — not to mention respectful dignified worship.[3]

We *must* strongly encourage Christians to engage in serious study, sharing, service, and worship! The leadership in the congregation must be responsible for setting this tone. We cannot overestimate the need for this to be done in the "average" congregation. It seems that many congregations still think that having a "teacher" go over the "standard, prepared lessons" a night or two before, and then "teaching" the class — which has done nothing at all to prepare — constitutes Christian education. If the average Christian starved his body the way he does his Christian mind or spirit, he would have been long since hospitalized or died from *severe* malnutrition.

True Christian education has to be saturated with

---

[3] See Miethe, *Living Your Faith*, pp. 93-98.

Serving Christ: A Family Affair

biblical content — with a serious study of what the Bible actually teaches. Christian education must fix in us a trust for His word. We are reminded of a most beautiful retelling of the story of Abraham and Sarah:

> And it was so.
> And I learned a lesson
> which kept me through many times of icy beasts—
> trust His word alone—
> never the sense of His presence only.
> The presence is strength and joy unspeakable,
> but perseverance comes with holding to His word.
> Embrace the promise.
> The presence comes and goes,
> but His word is a rock anchoring the soul.
> And in the end, the presence returns
> and He has been there all the time.[4]

Real Christian education must answer the *why* questions; i.e., the meaning questions, not just the *how*, *when*, or *where* ones. It is not enough to study, for example, the genealogies in the Bible, the kings and judges of the Old Testament, or the missionary journeys of the Apostle Paul. Yes, Christian education must use a method to convey this truth to the believer. It is both content and method, never one or the other.[5]

Broadly speaking there are always two approaches to

---

[4]"Abram" speaking from *Abraham & Sarah: A Reminiscence* by Kent D. Berg, 1989, p. 10.

[5]Christian education is that discipline that provides a balance between the theories and the practices of Christian learning. In general, this discipline includes: (1) the nature of C.E. (Definitions and the range of formal to informal instruction); (2) the foundations of C.E. (rudimentary truths from theology, to philosophy, educational psychology, and social science); (3) the process of C.E. (the dynamics of interpersonal relationships and the ministry of the Holy Spirit); and (4) the program of C.E. (recruitment/training, curriculum, and methodology). Christian education also supports the overarching goals of the Christian life, such as maturing in Christ while setting

The Family, Christian Education, and the World

education: (1) rote memory — learning "facts" and repeating them on a test or quiz. In this method a "student" is constantly "forced" to regurgitate, as close to "word for word" as is possible, what has been presented. This is not education. It is propaganda or indoctrination! Interestingly enough, this is what the communists called education.

Believe it or not student after student tells Terry that this is what is expected of them by most of their professors. While jokingly "complaining" that Terry requires his students to think on their exams, an older student who works in the registrar's office of the university she attends, said her high school education was harder, more demanding, than most of her university courses. Amazing! This is not education and ultimately it defeats the very thing it attempts to accomplish, i.e., to educate. This view of "education" as fill-in-the-blank, multiple choice, true or false answers; as rote memory and regurgitation is also contributing to our society's decline.

Education is more than dispelling ignorance, or pointing out "error." It must be about showing people the truth. How accurate that, "It is one thing to show a man that he is in error, and another to put him in possession of truth."[6] As Christians, *we* have an opportunity, and an obligation, to reveal not only the error, but to put people in possession of the Truth. As John 8:32 says, ". . . and you shall know the truth, and the truth shall make you free." Jesus is the Truth we must show to a lost and troubled world. We can only do this if we ourselves know Him and share that knowledge with others. This is an important role of the Christian family.

---

goals according to age-level appropriateness, holistic growth, and cross-cultural distinctiveness. Miethe, *The Compact Dictionary of Doctrinal Words*, pp. 57-58.

[6]Locke, *Essay Concerning Human Understanding*, Book IV, Ch. 7, Sec. 12.

(2) The second method of education is to take a rather small, systematically presented set of facts as a foundation, and use these to teach one how to think through a problem or situation. The student learns to analyze problems and synthesize material and deduce conclusions based on how the facts fit the situation. Certainly this is what Christian education must be about. Specifically, Christian education should assist the individual learner in his or her faith pilgrimage: (a) to know the "what and why" of his or her belief in truth; (b) to utilize that truth to choose (among alternatives) a personal value system; and (c) to appropriate his or her value system to life in such a way that it will produce the "fruit" of godly character.[7] Here, again, the Christian family is absolutely essential. Remember: There are only two divinely appointed institutions in the Bible — the home and the church. Christian education is of the greatest importance to both of these, for neither can stand without it!

The Family and the Home

The home can, and should be, one of the most important and vital aspects of the teaching ministry of the church. But for this to become a reality, we must implement the biblical theology of the home, employing our churches and our families for that purpose. We must be willing to ask a potentially painful question. Is it possible that our church programs, by constantly dividing families into age related groupings, etc., are doing more to destroy the biblical functions of the home than they are to nurture them? Often this is exactly the case.

The family unit is seen as important through what the Bible says about the home. The home is God's means for

---

[7]For useful references to the study of Christian Education see the short bibliography after the entry on "Christian Education" in *The Compact Dictionary of Doctrinal Words*, pp. 57-58.

The Family, Christian Education, and the World

procreation (Gen. 2:18-24). Marriage and sex are of God. Sex was given to man by God to be a foundation for the highest of physical relationships. A man and woman are united in marriage. Marriage is sacred! But the only way two people can grow closer to each other is by each growing closer to God. (Thanks again, Professor Bussmann!)

As we have seen, the Bible is very clear about the parents' responsibility to instruct their children in the home. Again, we quote Deuteronomy 6:4-9:

> Hear, O Israel! The Lord is our God, the Lord is one! And you shall love the Lord your God will all your heart and with all your soul and with all your might. And these words, which I am commanding you today, shall be on your heart; and you shall teach them diligently to your sons and shall talk to them when you sit in your house and when you walk by the way and when you lie down and when you rise up. And you shall bind them as a sign on your hand and they shall be as frontals on your forehead. And you shall write them on the doorposts of your house and on your gates.

The New Testament gives no indication that we are relieved of responsibility for this instruction. We all *must* imprint this on our minds and our doors. God's truth must be at the center of our consciousness; i.e., our minds or reasoning ability. And, it must be possessed or known with the repeated emphasis of habit.

The family is essential because of the Bible's teaching on learning as a direct responsibility of the home. Jesus taught by being aware and making others aware, not only of content, but of feelings and attitudes. He communicated not just formal teaching, although His teaching did include that element (Luke 11:1). Jesus also taught by participation. It was theory applied to the practical. "Involve me and I will understand." It was teaching in the fullest sense.

Serving Christ: A Family Affair

The biblical emphasis on learning in the home is quite natural, not only in light of God's plan for the family, but also in relation to practical considerations. The children should be under the control of the home, more than that of any other institution. The parents bear the responsibility and have the time, *if* they understand and set priorities, to be examples and establish experiences by participation. The church has the child one percent of the time. The school has the child 16 percent of the time and the home has the child 83 percent of the time — that is, if we do not give up our time in unwise aligning of priorities. Whatever possessed us to think that church educational programs could somehow substitute for the home in the task of Christian education? Or, do we not care?!

As Americans, we have more leisure time than ever before, and yet we all wonder "where the time goes." Again, it is a matter of priorities! If we would do less television watching, etc., we could better utilize the time we have our children for nurture in the Lord. We must realize that we have a responsibility to discipline our lives for Jesus! There is only one means of achievement for the maturing Christian — Christian education. Who is responsible for Christian education? First, the family, then the church.

Jewish children were nurtured in the Old Testament Scriptures and faith in God at home! A strong case can be made for the assertion that the Jewish people survived five thousand years only because of the nation's emphasis on education in the home. And, a case can be made that the final decay and judgment on the nation was a result of a lack of strong scriptural education in the home.

The Christian family is important as a model of what a family should be to society, as a witness to the Lord, and because of its responsibility in evangelism. For New Testament examples showing the family structure sustaining evangelism see the household conversions recorded

The Family, Christian Education, and the World

in the book of Acts (16:31-34). Evangelism through children[8] and the family unit is natural and biblical. We must do some rethinking in the Christian church about our responsibilities for using the assets of our families to win other families to our Lord! If our churches were first of all family oriented, perhaps we would again realize not only the place of the family in the church, but the importance of the family as a means of evangelism.

Where Do We Go From Here

Present world conditions demand renewed emphasis on *Christian education as a responsibility of the home — to take place in the home.* We are experiencing a rapid change in many cultures. Change in social structures always affect the home. Certainly, now we can see the result of post-World War II materialism in our culture and on our families. It has almost destroyed us as a nation. A whole generation of fathers and mothers wanted "to give their children all the *things* they never had." Especially under the threat of atomic destruction it was not a dishonorable goal. But it led to a permissive lack of discipline in all the social-economic and political areas of our society. These fathers and mothers often confused the giving of things with the giving of love or so mixed them that the children were almost fatally confused. It has almost destroyed us!

As Christians, what we do not know, we must *learn* — about our faith, about "being a parent," and about living in and witnessing to our world! What we know, we must

---

[8]We are not here advocating making our children into "hellfire and brimstone preachers" as I have known some fundamentalistic families to do. Rather, our children can be taught to love and to share their knowledge of the love of God quite naturally and kindly as a real part of who they are as young Christians. With them — as well as with their parents — what they model and how is perhaps more important than what they say.

Serving Christ: A Family Affair

practice! In the "Preface," we quoted Locke as saying that all people are liable, and most under temptation, to error by passion or interest. Many centuries before, Aristotle said for an "act" to be virtuous, (1) we must know what we are doing, (2) must deliberately choose to do it, and (3) must do it as a part of our own firm and immutable character. The great philosopher wrote:

> . . . most people, instead of acting, take refuge in theorizing, they imagine that they are philosophers and that philosophy will make them virtuous; in fact, they behave like people who listen attentively to their doctors but never do anything that their doctors tell them. But a healthy state of the soul will no more be produced by this kind of philosophizing than a healthy state of the body by this kind of medical treatment.

Most people today, it seems, could care less about (are "too busy" for) either "theory" or family "action." Christians must embody both "content" and "deed." "We must also note the weaknesses to which we are ourselves particularly prone," said Aristotle.[9] As Christians, we must "prove [our]selves doers of the word, and not merely hearers who delude themselves" (James 1:22).

In response to our world, a Christian home can be and should be a powerful witness to the fundamental truth of Christianity and of lasting values. We, the individuals

---

[9]Aristotle (384-322 B.C.), *Nicomachean Ethics*, Book II, Chapters 3 and 9 reprinted in Louis P. Pojman, *Philosophy: The Quest for Truth* (Belmont, CA: Wadsworth Publishing Company, 1992), pp. 354, 357. Christians would do well to remember that *truth* is truth no matter where it is found. Sometimes we can more effectively use truth from a "secular" source, rather than trying to make our point by "beating" someone over the head with the Bible, and alienating them in the process. See Miethe, "Plato's Metaphysics: His Contribution to a Philosophy of God," in *Taking Every Thought Captive: Essays in Honor of James D. Strauss*, edited by John Castelein & Richard Knopp, forthcoming from College Press.

The Family, Christian Education, and the World

who make up the families, which in turn make up our churches, must put biblical directives in control of our lives. The family unit can and should be the foundation and building block of a Christ-influenced society. Christian families are salt in the general society (Matt. 5:13; Col. 4:5-6); and we are *members* of one another in the Christian community, the body of Christ. Being "in Christ" must truly enlarge our family circle (Mark 3:35; 1 Tim. 5:1-3).

If history teaches us anything, it should remind us that Christ is glorified and the church grows through adversity. But growth is extremely hard if the adversity is coming from *within* the church! We *must* learn to pull together! We must also learn that as we encounter more pressure from a society run amuck, we no longer have the "luxury" of the time to waste our resources fighting among ourselves. [10] Hallelujah! *It is about time we stopped fighting among ourselves* (John 17)! When we think of some of the issues that brothers in Christ are fighting over; so petty and ridiculous when seen for what they are, and in the context of the message of the Gospel; they make us greatly saddened and truly ashamed. It is no wonder so many people have such a bad view of churches.

The church can do much to strengthen the home and

---

[10]Terry tried to make this point in "A Vision for the Church" in *One Body*, Vol. 11, No. 3 (Summer 1994), 11-13. "What I said was that the students I have taught, some of the very best in several of the Churches of Christ universities, do not care much about the issues that have long divided the two fellowships; e.g., the pros or cons of instrumental music, etc. I also said that they do not have the 'luxury' of spending time fighting over such issues when both of our groups — for the most part — are dying. They realize that we cannot defend most of what we have been arguing about (supposedly) from Scripture; that, in fact, we have put what were 'side issues' at best on 'center stage' where they never should have been and most certainly are not in the New Testament."

reestablish this powerful force for world evangelism. We must stop robbing the home of the time it needs to function. Elders and ministers need to educate Christian parents about the responsibilities of discipleship and nurture in the home. We need a strong program of adult education in the church which will permeate the home and reach the world (Matt. 18:19-20). Unquestionably, strengthened family ties will reduce the generation gap and improve the general health of society.

Christian education and the Christian family must relate to the world. The Bible teaches that the basic unit for Christian teaching — for any teaching — is the family, and the family is the basic unit for building the church and civilization. *Knowing and sharing the riches of God's wisdom (Phil. 1:9-11, John 8:31-32, 1 Cor. 4:1-2) by and through the Christian family, then, has to be the key to building the faith — to evangelism — in the world today! Why haven't we seen this?*

What could be more natural to a family, or a church, that makes a total commitment to God by formal and informal instruction, than service or ministry for Christ? The most natural way in the world to serve or minister is to make your service or ministry such an integral — that is, necessary for completeness — part of your everyday life that it becomes indistinguishable from other parts of that life. Christianity is not a way of life, it *is* life. If we are not living as Christians, we are not living, we are only existing.

Thus, the Christian home must be a powerful witness to biblical truth, a building block of a Christ-influenced society, and the key to biblical evangelism in any age. When every member in every family in the church comes to realize that his or her home may and must reflect the beauty and glow of His perfect love, *serving Christ will truly be a family affair!*

Epilogue
The Family, Ministry, and the Future

Where we are, Christ is. That is ministry! Thank the Lord that the "Me Generation" is — hopefully — finally over! One of the surest tests of whether one is a disciple or not is, in fact, if that person is "discipling." The non-discipling disciple is a contradiction by definition. It is true that Christians should witness by example, but there comes a time when a witness needs to be verbalized as well. "Ministry is the glorious privilege and serious responsibility of *every man, woman, and child who claims the name of Christ*. Witnessing, loving, sharing themselves and their possessions, are essential ways ministry is expressed by individual Christians."[1]

You claim to be a Christian. Do you see yourself as a minister of Christ? You should. In fact, you should have realized this when you accepted Him as Savior and Lord of our life. We believe, we know, that God has a purpose for your life. Discover it, strive to fulfill it, and you will be the richest of persons! But remember, striving should be done with patience. In the race to be better or best, miss not the joy of being.

We can be afraid of the world and of knowledge, and many of us are! But *the world is still God's world*, His creation. As Christians, *we* must take a place of responsibility in it, and for it! Locke said, "The only fence against the world is a thorough knowledge of it."[2] And, as Terry

---

[1] Miethe, *Reflections*, Vol. 1, 1980.
[2] Locke, *Some Thoughts Concerning Education*, Sec. 88.

Serving Christ: A Family Affair

has reflected (as a result of our experience), "Many people fear education. And certainly education can be misused. But I fear its opposite far more! After all, the only way to combat the misuse of education is to know! (John 8:32)"[3]

Christians, the only way to minimize the negative effects of the fallen world around us is to *know*, both His word and our world, and to be responsible enough to take our proper place in it. How else can we be salt, light, and leaven? In any generation if we, as Christians, are to lead and/or impact the society in which we live, we must be willing to: (1) Be radically committed to God. Christians must realize their self-worth and very being comes from knowledge and experience of God. And (2), we must form intimate communities in which we live in loving relation to one another and not as individuals caught up in personal priorities, prejudice, or petty ego.

Much earlier, we said that in accepting Christ as Savior it is very often hard to get it through our heads that we have been forgiven, to truly accept psychologically the reality of His forgiveness of our sins. This may be complicated by the church. One of the real problems in many churches is that people are not very forgiving. Often, we simply do not allow people to learn from their mistakes. To *grow* is often, perhaps most often, a positive aspect of learning by or through a mistake. "Maturity" is almost essentially the result of learning through mistakes! What is a "church" *if* it is not a place that understands this? It is most important that you find for yourself a loving and forgiving community of believers for support, fellowship, and sharing.

If people are healthy in Christ, they do not have any choice but to be priests. Christenson says it well:

> Father! Mother! God has called you to be priests unto

---

[3]Miethe, *Reflections*, Vol. II (1983).

Epilogue

your children. Through that priesthood, Jesus will enter into the life and experience of your home. And already here upon earth, you and your children will experience a foretaste of heaven. "For this is eternal life, that they know thee the only true God, and Jesus Christ whom thou has sent" (John 17:3).[4]

Surely we have established that the church has a responsibility to help the family face the future. The future may not be ours to see, but it is ours to make! The church is portrayed in Scripture as a transformed community. The church is a body within which believers minister to one another in such a way that individually and corporately there is growth in Christlikeness. Ephesians 4:13-16 tells us that we should strive to:

> ... attain to the unity of the faith, and of the knowledge of the Son of God, to a mature man, to the measure of the stature which belongs to the fullness of Christ. As a result, we are no longer to be children tossed here and there by waves, and carried about by every wind of doctrine, by the trickery of men, by craftiness in deceitful scheming; but speaking the truth in love, we are to grow up in all aspects into Him, who is the head, even Christ, from whom the whole body, being fitted and held together by that which every joint supplies, according to the proper working of each individual part, causes the growth of the body for the building up of itself in love.

Amen! This is the job of the family and the church working together! "The notion that husband, wife, and children are a complete unit, having no need for support from without, is one of the romanticized fictions of secular society; it is not biblical."[5]

---

[4]Christenson, *The Christian Family*, pp. 196-197.

[5]Larry Richards, "How the Church Can Help the Family Face the Future" in Collins' *Facing the Future*, p. 12.

Serving Christ: A Family Affair

If the church is going to help the family face the future it must emphasize the Body of Christ as a transforming community. A "dead" social club going by the name of First _____ Church will not help her families, nor in actuality the community very much either. In recognizing the importance of the family, the church must see itself as an extension of the family, existing for the family as a support mechanism — not just as a little business trying to become a bigger one, or a big business trying to become even bigger. The church must "develop approaches to family ministry which *incarnate* rather than simply *verbalize* a family-enriching way of life."[6]

For nearly the last two decades, Americans have been caught up in a "fitness" craze. However, now we hear that more Americans are overweight and out of shape than ever before. The human body is a wonderful thing, a genuinely miraculous organism. It is truly amazing that it can "maintain itself" with the daily neglect most of us visit upon it. Not only the abuse of drugs, including alcohol and cigarettes, but the daily lack of proper nutrition and exercise and unnecessary stress, yet, it still serves us for many years. We would be much better off if we bear in mind that "a sound mind in a sound body, is a short, but full description of a happy state in this world."[7]

The family is also a miraculous organism when you think about it. We abuse it in unimaginable ways — sometimes in the name of Christianity — and even mortally wound it. Nevertheless, it seems often capable of survival and, even after we think it dead, of resuscitation. We are convinced that most families really do want to

---

[6]Larry Richards, "How the Church Can Help the Family Face the Future," p. 14.

[7]Locke, *Some Thoughts on Education* (1693), Sec. 1. Long before Locke, Decimus Junius Juvenal (c. A.D. 50-130) said, "You should pray for a sound mind in a sound body." *Satires* X, 356, *Mens sana in corpore sano*.

Epilogue

survive, even though many simply don't know how. This, again, screams out the need for the church to restructure itself with the family in mind and for individual Christian families to realize their proper place as a ministry team.

We would do well to start a "family fitness craze" in America. Just as with the individual body, when nourished and exercised properly, begin to imagine how glorious a healthy family can be, especially when Christ is its head. And, if Christ is the head of our family, how can it help but serve, or minister! There is nothing on earth more fulfilling or *more exciting* than a family immersed in God, sharing the very love and character of God with people who need that love and character for life itself (both for this world and the next). *Serving Christ as a family is the hope of the church and of our society*! No question about it.

Mark 3:35 tells us that Jesus said, "whoever does the will of God, he is My brother and sister and mother." The early church described throughout the New Testament embodied those distinguishing marks which we long for today in our families: enduring love; interdependence; stability; loyalty and devotion; commitment and responsibility; security in time of change, of crisis, and of old age. This should be the family of God of which all believers are a part! Yes, individual families need to become families again. But with the millions of sick and seriously wounded — as if the result of some great war flung in all directions, in dysfunctional and "partial" families or no family at all — the church today must reach out to and minister to these "war" ravaged children of God.

If we in God's family, God's own very children, cannot through the power of Christ build healthy families, bridges across generations, and family ministries to those in need; how can we expect the rest of society to be successful? *We* (all of us in the church) hold the key to a

Serving Christ: A Family Affair

revolutionary model of love and hope for our society, if we will only venture out of the box. Empowered by the Holy Spirit with love for one another, we can face the problems of life and relationships anew and find answers together.

Neither the "world" nor we, as Christians, can claim "ignorance" as an excuse. As Paul told the Romans:

> For the wrath of God is revealed from heaven against all ungodliness and unrighteousness of men, who suppress the truth in unrighteousness, because that which is known about God is evident within them; for *God made it evident to them. For since the creation of the world His invisible attributes, His eternal power and divine nature, have been clearly seen, being understood though what has been made, so that they are without excuse.* For even though they knew God they did not honor Him as God, or give thanks; but they became futile in their speculations, and their foolish heart was darkened. Professing to be wise, they became fools . . . (1:18-22, emphasis added).

The Scripture then goes on to tell us plainly about their foolishness (23-33). Sounds very much like our world today! Ignorance is *not* an excuse, not for "them" and not for us! Even those who have never heard the gospel (who in one sense are totally secular) have within them a witness of the goodness of God. Let us, as Christians, never be a cause of hiding the goodness and the love of God from others so that *we* can be used as an excuse.

The American family is not well! But the cure will not come by us just setting around and wringing our hands over the problem. *The answer must be for Christian families once again to take their place in the church and society as models and ministers.* We must practice and model love and discipline. We must show the families of the world how wonderful it is, what great fun it is, to be a Christian family! Pray for our family as we pray for yours. "Life can

Epilogue

only be understood backwards, but it must be lived forwards."[8] Through Christ in a real sense, we must make the future! We would do very well to ponder, "It seems a great distance but it is very short — but a step from the cradle to the grave, from earth to heaven, from time to eternity!"[9] We hope that you, and yours, will always bear in *mind*:

>God undergirds you.
>God sustains you.
>God empowers you.
>God strengthens you
>God loves you.
>Live for God,
>Because you desire nothing less
>And you request nothing more;
>Through His Son, our Savior. Amen.[10]

May your family be HIS family!

---

[8]Søren Kierkegaard, *Stages on Life's Way*. Translated by W. Lowrie (Princeton, NJ: Princeton University Press, 1940).

[9]Alexander Campbell, *The Millennial Harbinger* (1866), p. 137.

[10]E. Lee Phillips, *Prayers for Worship* (Waco, TX: Word Books, 1979), p. 135.

Select Bibliography

Anderson, Ray S., and Dennis B. Guernsey. *On Being Family: Essays on a Social Theology of the Family.* Grand Rapids: Eerdmans, 1986.

Blankenhorn, David, *et al.*, eds. *Rebuilding the Nest: A New Commitment to the American Family.* Milwaukee: Family Services America, 1991.

Boyer, Ernest. *Finding God at Home: Family Life as Spiritual Discipline.* San Francisco: Harper & Row, 1988.

Christenson, Larry. *The Christian Family.* Minneapolis: Bethany House Publishers, 1970.

Collins, Gary R. *Facing the Future: The Church and Family Together.* Waco: Word Books, 1976.

_____, ed. *Living & Growing Together: The Christian Family Today.* Waco: Word Books, 1976.

_____, ed. *Make More of Your Marriage.* Waco: Word Books, 1976.

Edelman, Marian Wright. *Families in Peril: An Agenda for Social Change.* Cambridge, MA: Harvard University Press, 1987.

Gangel, Kenneth O. *The Family First: Biblical Answers to Family Problems.* Minneapolis: His International Service, 1972. Reissued rev. ed. Winona Lake, IN: BMH Books, 1979.

_____, and Elizabeth Gangel. *Between Christian Parent and Child.* Grand Rapids: Baker Book House, 1974.

Gerber, Jerry, Janet Wolff, Walter Klores, and Gene Brown. *Lifetrends: The Future of Baby Boomers and Other Aging Americans.* New York: Macmillan, 1989.

Hearn, Virginia, ed. *What They Did Right: Reflections on Parents by Their Children.* Wheaton, IL: Tyndale House Publishers, 1974.

Horton, Anne L., ed. *Abuse and Religion: When Praying Isn't Enough.* Lexington, MA: Lexington Books, 1988.

LaHaye, Tim and Beverly. *The Act of Marriage: The Beauty of Sexual Love.* Grand Rapids: Zondervan, 1976.

McKay, Bobbie. *What Ever Happened to the Family?* Cleveland: Pilgrim Press, 1992.

Mayo, Mary Ann. *A Christian Guide to Sexual Counseling: Recovering the Mystery and Reality of "One Flesh."* Grand Rapids: Zondervan, 1987.

Melton, J. Gordon, ed. *The Churches Speak on Sex and Family Life.* Detroit: Gale Research, 1991.

Miethe, Terry L. *A Believer's Guide to Essential Christianity.* Joplin, MO: College Press Publishing Company, forthcoming.

_____. *Living Your Faith: Closing the Gap Between Mind and Heart.* Joplin, MO: College Press Publishing Company, 1993.

Napier, Augustus Y. *The Fragile Bond.* New York: Harper & Row, 1988.

Patton, John. *Christian Marriage and Family.* Nashville: Abingdon Press, 1988.

Powell, John. *The Secret of Staying in Love.* Niles, IL: Argus Communications, 1974.

Shedd, Charlie W. *Letters to Karen: On Keeping Love in Marriage.* Nashville: Abingdon Press, a Spire Book, 1965.

_____. *Letters to Philip: On How to Treat a Woman*. Old Tappan, NJ: Fleming H. Revell Company, a Spire Book, 1968.

_____. *You Can Be a Great Parent!* Waco: Word Books, 1982.

Williams, Norman V. *The Christian Home*. Chicago: Moody Press, 1952.

Wilt, Joy. *An Uncomplicated Guide to Becoming a Super-Parent** (A normal human being who knows how to behave so that both parent *and* child live happy, fulfilled lives.) Waco: Word Books, 1980.

Wright, H. Norman. *Communication: Key to Your Marriage*. Ventura, CA: Regal Books, 1974.

_____. *More Communication Keys for Your Marriage*. Ventura, CA: Regal Books, 1983.

_____. *The Pillars of Marriage*. Ventura, CA: Regal Books, 1979.

_____. *Seasons of a Marriage*. Ventura, CA: Regal Books, 1982.

Wright, Wendy M. *Sacred Dwelling: A Spirituality of Family Life*. New York: Crossroad, 1989.

Zimmerman, Carle C. and Lucius F. Cervantes. *Marriage and the Family: A Text for Moderns*. Chicago: Henry Regnery Company, 1965.

About the Authors

TERRY L. MIETHE is currently a postdoctoral fellow in history at Christ Church, the University of Oxford, England. Dr. Miethe holds the A.B. from Lincoln Christian College, the M.A. from Trinity Evangelical Divinity School, the M.Div. from McCormick Theological Seminary, the Ph.D. in philosophy (Phi Beta Kappa) from Saint Louis University, and the A.M. and Ph.D. in social ethics and theology from the University of Southern California. He has been a visiting professor at colleges and universities in the United States, Canada, and Europe. Dr. Miethe is a member of eight scholastic honor societies in philosophy, history, psychology, classical languages, and English, including Phi Beta Kappa and Alpha Sigma Nu. Dr. Miethe's books have been translated into German, Spanish, Korean, and Russian. He has also contributed eight articles for the *Dictionary of Christianity in America*, as well as articles and chapters in numerous other magazines and books.

BEVERLY J. MIETHE is Teacher of Special Education at Kenley School, Abilene, Texas and Associate Adjunct Professor of Education and Christian Education at Emmanuel College, Oxford. Mrs. Miethe holds the A.B. from Lincoln Christian College and the M.S. in Special Education/Learning Handicapped from the University of La Verne. She has studied at several colleges and universities in the United States and in England. Mrs. Miethe has lifetime multiple subject teaching certification, preschool through adult, in California and lifetime certification in general education in Missouri, as well as certification in Virginia and Texas. She has taught in public and private schools in Missouri, California, Virginia, and Texas.

Terry and Beverly met in grade school, were high school sweethearts, and have been very happily married for 26 years. The Miethes have ministered with churches in Indiana, Illinois, California, Virginia, and Texas. Terry has preached in several countries around the world. Their son, John Hayden, is married to Lisa Nicole. John and Nicole have one son, Britain Avery Miethe, to whom this book is dedicated.

BLUEFIELD COLLEGE OF EVANGELISM
LIBRARY
BLUEFIELD, W. VA. 24701